Directions 〉 1

Ina Taylor

Published in 2002 by:
Nelson Thornes Ltd
Delta Place
27 Bath Road
CHELTENHAM
GL53 7TH
United Kingdom

02 03 04 05 06 / 10 9 8 7 6 5 4 3 2 1

A catalogue record for this book is available from the British Library

ISBN 0 7487 6387 2

Illustrations by Lisa Berkshire and Angela Lumley

Design and page make-up by eMC Design

Printed and bound in China by Midas

Acknowledgements

With thanks to the following for permission to reproduce photographs and other copyright material in this book:

A Rocha: 110; Advertising Archive: 14; Andes Press Agency/Carlos Reyes Manzo: 73, 124; ARC: 119, 120/121, 125; Art Directors & Trip Photo Library: 19, 24, 60, 65, 67, 88; Associated Press: 17, 41, 42, 100 (right), 114; Bridgeman art Library: 108; Circa Photo Library: 76, 77; Clearvision Trust: 95, 99; The Fitzwilliam Museum: 7; Fortean Picture Library: 11; John Birdsall Photography: 37; Ecoscene/Martin Lillicrap: 118; Ecoscene/Sally Morgan: 106; Phil Emmett: 72; Kobal Collection: 26; M.C.Escher's "Relativity" © 2001 Cordon Art B.V.-Baarn-Holland. All Rights Reserved: 8; Network Photographers: 122; Noah Project: 113; Press Association: 18, 25, 33, 39, 84; Rex Features: 15, 29, 45, 90, 96, 103 (bottom inset); Rex Features/Chris Harris: 54; Rex Features/Geoff Wilkinson: 38; Rex Features/Neil Higginson: 30; Rex Features/Sipa: 16, 43 (right), 47; Science Photo Library: 12; R.J.L.Smith: 44; Sonia Halliday Photos: 22; Still Pictures: 61; Taraloka: 98; Ina Taylor: 27, 28, 55, 56, 70, 75, 78, 79, 80, 86 (both), 93, 100 (left), cover (bottom right); Telegraph Picture Library: 69; Topham Picturepoint: 35, 103 (middle inset); Topham Picturepoint/Dave Cheskin: 32; Topham Picturepoint/Tony Melville: 116

Every effort has been made to contact copyright holders. The publishers apologise to anyone whose rights have been inadvertently overlooked, and will be happy to rectify any errors or omissions.

Contents

Unit 1 ▷ Where do we look for God?

What do they say about God?

I saw God the other day. I did really.

I just looked up and there he was, sitting on the edge of a cloud, dangling his legs.

I said, 'Hello God, how are you?'

'Not so bad,' he said. 'How'd you know it was me?'

I said, 'Well, I just guessed, really. Seeing you sitting up there on a cloud – wasn't anyone else it could be.'

'Rubbish,' said God. 'Could've been anybody – spaceman, steeplejack, window-cleaner, lift-attendant – anybody with a head for heights.'

'Yes, but not just sitting up there on a cloud,' I said.

He was quiet for a minute – thinking. Then he moved round and propped himself up on his elbows and peered at me over the edge of the cloud.

'What else?' he said.

'Well, you look like God,' I said, 'with that old wrinkled face and long white beard. You're what I've always imagined you to be. Who else could you be?'

'Father Christmas,' he suggested.

'Don't be daft,' I said. 'Nobody believes in Father Christmas.'

'Does anyone believe in me?' he asked.

'Well,' I said, 'some do, some don't.'

So he asked, 'Those who do – what do they say?'

'They look at the world,' I said, ' and they see the beauty and order of nature, and they reckon it couldn't have happened by accident. Must be God.'

'I see,' said God. 'And those who don't.'

'They look at the world as well, ' I told him. 'They look at war and human misery, homelessness, pollution. They reckon if God existed, it wouldn't happen.'

'I see,' said God. 'You know their trouble, don't you? It's not me they don't believe in, it's themselves. I mean to say, I've given them the power to put it right. They just won't use it.'

'What power is that?' I said.

'They know right from wrong,' he said. 'That's all they need.'

'Not willpower?' I asked.

'Ah,' he said, and I'm certain he winked at me. 'They have to ask for that.'

'Ask for it?'

'Well, I can't give to them if they don't want it,' he said. 'It'd be like stepping in and clearing up the mess myself. I couldn't do that now, could I?'

'Why not?' I asked him.

'Well…,' he said, and he winked again, and smiled, 'It'd leave them nothing to do, wouldn't it? They'd have such an easy time of it, they still wouldn't believe in me.'

Then he disappeared, and I thought about what he had said, and I remembered the smile and the wink, and wondered if he was joking.

Suddenly, he came back. He stood on the cloud, his face like thunder. He cupped his hands, and he called out to the world below…

'BESIDES – IT'S YOUR MESS!'

from *So God Said To Me*, Richard Adams

The story begins with a child's idea of God.

- List the points that show this.

- Add some things people said about God when you were younger.

- The story is obviously a bit of fun but it has a point. What is it saying about the way people look at the world around them?

- Is the word God helpful? Or does it make you think of the old man with the beard idea? Would you find it easier to just think in terms of a power, or force, that is greater than you?

- Hindus talk of God as 'the Ultimate Reality'. What words would you find helpful?

Is it wrong to write a story like this about God? Do you feel comfortable with pictures of God even though nobody knows what God looks like?

This famous painting is called *God creating the Universe*.

- With a partner, list the things William Blake, the artist, is trying to say about God.

- What are the similarities between this picture and the story on the opposite page?

 Continue the dialogue between God and somebody. This time discuss the flood on page 116 which was probably caused by global warming.

Does God exist?

As it said in the story on page 6 'some do and some don't' believe in God.

A person who believes in God is called a **monotheist**. *Mono* means 'one' and *theist* means 'god' in Greek. From Greek again comes the word for a person who doesn't believe in any god, an **atheist**. *A* means 'without', so atheist means 'without god'. The words may be new to you but the ideas are simple. Yes, there is a god. No, there isn't a god.

Not everybody is so certain. Some people say, 'There may be a god but it is difficult to know'. A person who says 'maybe' is called **agnostic**, which means 'without knowledge'.

Is seeing believing?

The idea of God sitting up in the sky on a cloud might have been acceptable for ancient people but it was silly once people could travel into space. Does anyone really expect to 'see' God anyway?

- Write a couple of sentences to explain what 'seeing is believing' means.

- What would a magician like David Copperfield or Paul Daniels say about the idea that 'seeing is believing'?

- When we say, 'You could cut the atmosphere with a knife', what do we mean? Can you see anything then? How do you know what's going on?

- In pairs make a list of six things you cannot see, but believe exist.

- Even if the cleverest brain surgeon in the world looked inside a person's head, he would not see an idea. Does that mean there is no such thing as an idea?

- Do you have to see something to believe in it? What about feelings? Can you see love or warmth? Or is it just the effect that you see?

LOOKING BACK

Look back at the title page of this unit. Why were those images chosen?

Is seeing believing? Or can we be tricked?

Is there anybody out there?

Some say God is all around us on the outside, even though we cannot see anything. Others believe God is a part of everything and so will be found on the inside. There are others who believe God is both inside and outside everything. One group of Christians, called Quakers, say there is 'that of God in everyone'. They believe each person has a bit of good in him, even the worst criminal. You may call it goodness or you might call it God. They do not believe there is any difference.

Humanists do not think it is ever possible to find evidence of whether God exists or not. They do not think it matters either. They are sure that people can lead happy, fulfilled lives, and help others to, without a god. Humanists could be agnostic or atheist.

Yuri Gagarin was the first man to be sent into space on 12 April 1961. When he came back he said that he did not see God when he was out in space. He was joking but why do you think he said it?

ACTIVITY **A**

- Write a story based on the title 'Seeing is believing'. Your story could prove that seeing is believing, or you could include a twist in it so that seeing is not believing after all.

- Design your own title page in your exercise book and choose the best images you can think of for this work. Would a Wanted poster for God work better?

- Make a poster on a double page in your book or on paper. Show the different views of monotheists, atheists, agnostics and humanists.

Prove it!

This computer is linked to the Internet and uses a very powerful search engine. Ask it any question you like because it has access to the largest knowledge bank in the world.

- In pairs make up ten difficult questions you would like this computer to answer.

- In pairs look at the ten questions for the computer. Pick out any that you think the computer will not be able to answer. Why will the cleverest computer in the world not know the answer?

Questions for the computer:

1 What is the population of the capital city in Japan?
2 How many stars are in the universe?
3 When was my grandmother born?
4 What is the chemical symbol for potassium?
5 Is pink a better colour than green?
6 When did the dodo become extinct?
7 What do brussel sprouts taste like?
8 In what year will I get married?
9 Why do people suffer pain?
10 How do I know if I am in love?

Who do you trust?

- Who do you trust most to give you a truthful answer?

- Look at the list on the right and put it in the order of the one you would trust most first, down to the one you would least trust at the bottom. You can add three more possible sources if you wish.

Information given:

- on a computer
- in an encyclopaedia
- by your mum
- by a teacher
- on television
- by your best friend
- in a newspaper
- through your own eyes.

This photograph of a fairy is a hoax but many people thought it was scientific proof a hundred years ago.

In pairs write three arguments that prove the Earth is round. Now make up three arguments to 'prove' the Earth is flat. This is not as difficult as you may think. Chances are that nobody in the class has seen the Earth with their own eyes from outer space. Most of us take it on trust.

Are the photographs we have seen of a round earth a hoax, like pictures of fairies? When people sail off into the distance and disappear, they might have fallen over the edge of the Earth.

With your partner design a questionnaire to find out how trusting people are. You will need a series of questions. You could plan this as a spreadsheet if you wish.

To make it easy to collect data, offer four possible answers for each question. Try to cover different things a person might take on trust. For example:

- Do you trust that someone cares about you if you do not often see them?

- Would you let someone borrow something valuable?

- Would you loan money?

- Would you trust a nurse to do the best for you?

- Would you go mountain-climbing roped to someone else? etc.

Wow!

It takes your breath away!

- Think of a situation when you were taken by complete surprise by what you saw. What did this feel like? Perhaps if you expected something impressive, it would have been a disappointment. List a few things that have impressed you.

- Have you ever been totally overawed by a car, some clothes, being in a crowd at a concert or a football match?

- Go through your list and sort it into the things that were made by people and those that were natural. Your second list might be longer than your first. It seems that things which occur in nature amaze us most.

Things that make a profound impression on us can be quite personal. Your list is unique to you and definitely not for reading out to the class. Your list might include a wide range: the view from the top of a hill one warm sunny day; being in love; watching your cat give birth to kittens; seeing the eclipse; standing alongside a jumbo jet.

Through the centuries it has been the natural world that has inspired artists, musicians, sculptors and poets the most. They responded to nature by creating something themselves. For some people it is their encounter with the natural world that convinces them there must be some force that is greater than us.

Do you think a computer program could have that effect on someone?

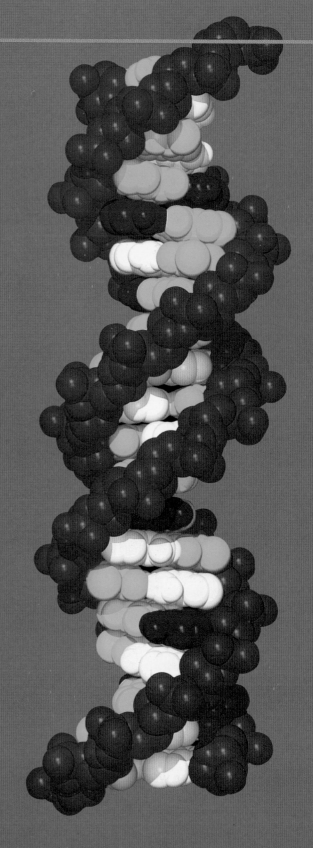

Scientists have worked out that this is the DNA pattern of life. Scientists did not invent it. In fact it has taken them hundreds of years to be able to see it yet the pattern has been there since the beginning of time. Did anyone design it or did it happen by chance?

This is the galaxy we call the Milky Way. Astronomers think there are a hundred thousand million stars in this galaxy alone. Can you imagine what that looks like? Can you write it in numbers? Scientists also think there are probably about the same number of galaxies out there! This means that every human being on the planet could own twenty galaxies each. Imagine that!

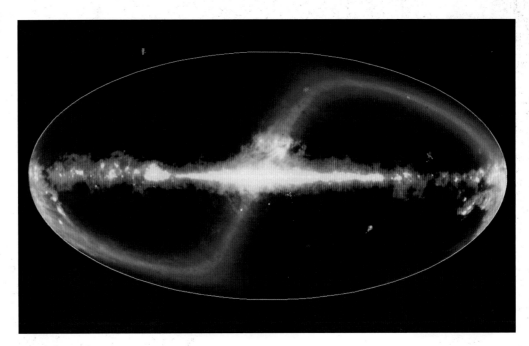

How clearly the sky reveals God's glory!
How plainly it shows what he has done!
Each day announces it to the following day:
Each night repeats to the next.
No speech or words are used, no sound is heard;
Yet their message goes out to all the world and is heard to the ends of the earth.

> Psalm 19:1–4 from the Jewish and Christian scriptures

Do you not see how God drives the clouds, then gathers and piles them up in masses which pour down torrents of rain? From heaven's mountains He sends down the hail, pelting with it whom He will and turning it away from whom He pleases. The flashes of His lightning almost snatches off men's eyes.

> from the Muslim holy book *The Qur'an* 24:43

God created the night, the seasons, days of the month and week.
He created the wind, water, fire and the worlds below...
He the Creator, beholds His creation and looks upon it with grace.
Here there are continents, worlds and universes.
Who can describe a boundless bound?
Here there are worlds within worlds and endless forms.

> from the Sikh hymn *The Japji*

ACTIVITY A

- **Look in magazines and colour supplements for pictures you think are great. Cut them out and put them on a poster entitled 'Wow!' Try to make it as varied as possible. Select some quotations from holy writings to add to the poster. They can be ones on this page or others you find.**

- **Compose your own poem to celebrate an aspect of the natural world. Or, if you prefer, paint a scene to celebrate the natural world.**

The ultimate designer label

Look at the clothes you are wearing now and all the things in your schoolbag. Someone must have designed every single item, even if most people would not call their school uniform designer gear. Items do not create themselves. Every product will have been drawn up in just the same way you begin a project in Design and Technology. Some people say the world could not have just happened on its own. There must have been a designer or creator. They say that this proves there is a god.

CK
Calvin Klein Jeans

Black Selvage

The ultimate fashion accessory is a designer label. Many people think it is more than just a label. It says something about the person who wears it. Designer clothes are thought to be better than ordinary ones because talented people planned them. Could you spot a designer garment even if the label was hidden?

When I look at the sky, which you have made, at the moon and the stars, which you have set in their places – what is man, that you think of him; mere man, that you care for him?

This is a very expensive designer watch. In the eighteenth century a philosopher called Paley told a story about a watch. He said if somebody was walking in a field and found a watch lying in the grass, if that person had never seen a watch before then when he opened the back he would be amazed at its tiny intricate works. He would know that the watch had been made by a clever person. He would never think that watch happened by accident. Paley said the same is true of the world which is far more complicated than a watch mechanism. What do you think?

Whoops!

- Could the whole universe be the result of an accident? If God did not design it deliberately, could it just happen? With a partner work out three reasons people might give for creation being an accident.

- Now work out three reasons somebody might give for creation being deliberate.

There is an endless question behind the idea of a God who designs things. Who designed God? Who designed the person who designed God?

 GOING FORWARD
In unit 1.6 there is another question about the ultimate designer.

- Write at least two sentences to explain what is meant by God, the designer of the world.

- Would an atheist be convinced by the watch story? What reasons would they give?

- Does the argument convince you? Why?

 ACTIVITY A

- Role-play a discussion between the person who found the watch and an atheist.

- Design a logo with an appropriate sentence for God's designer label to go on parts of creation.

Why does this happen?

The scenes on these pages are in total contrast to the one on page 27. There the natural world is so beautiful and complex that people turn to God the creator. The name of God would certainly be used in the earthquake below.

LOOKING BACK

Look back at the ideas about the designer God on the previous pages. Can you see any problems with that idea of God and the scenes on these two pages?

This is the result of an earthquake that hit San Salvador in 2001. In fact there were two quakes only weeks apart. Many people were killed in the first quake. Most people died when they were trapped as buildings collapsed. Who was responsible for the earthquake?

In pairs work out answers to the following questions:

- **What would people say about God this time, do you think?**

- **Would the person buried in rubble waiting for a rescuer think of God?**

- **What would the rescuer who finds that person alive after three days say about God?**

- **What would the father of the dead child pulled out of the rubble say about God?**

- **Do you think most people involved would think about God at a time like this, or not?**

Why does this sort of terrorist incident happen? With a partner discuss whether God can be blamed for this? Give at least two reasons for your answer. Report back to the class.

Group work

- List the arguments for and against a designer God.
- Use pictures and stories you found in the newspapers to give your opinion about why things go wrong in the world.

ACTIVITY A Look through copies of a local or national newspaper. Cut out as many stories as you can that show the world is not always wonderful and beautiful.

- Analyse each story. Who do you think was to blame for what happened?

- Insurance companies use the term 'an act of God' when an event happens that they will not pay out on. A person might be killed by lightning or an earthquake could happen, like the one here. What do they mean by 'an act of God'? Write down two more events that might be called 'acts of God'. Would you say God is responsible?

Who started it?

GOING FORWARD →
In Unit 5 there are creation stories from various religious traditions as well as Humanism. Many of them share the idea that the world had a creator; it is the designer God concept again. Do you think the idea of God the creator could fit in with the scientific theory of creation?

Most of us have discovered that events do not usually happen by themselves. Anthony walked by the cupboard just as a pile of books fell out. He said, 'I didn't do anything. It just happened.' Did he tell the truth? Anthony believed he did. Dave threw the books in the cupboard earlier and did not bother to stack them, but it was the vibration Anthony made as he walked by that shook the books enough to make the whole lot fall out.

This was the world record attempt for toppling dominoes in August 1998. 1.6 million dominoes went down in Leeuworden, Netherlands. It took 100 people over 10 weeks to plan this. The record was broken in 2001. The movement of the dominoes could not have happened without someone starting them. It was all planned. Could this hold a clue to how the universe was created? Could God be the one who planned the Big Bang?

Sikhs wear a circular steel bracelet as a symbol that God is eternal. It is impossible to find where a circle begins and where it ends. Sikhs believe this is a symbol that God has no beginning and will never come to an end.

Choose one from the list below.

- Write a story
- Work out a role-play
- Make a poster to show the idea in cartoon form.

Show what caused the action and the effect the action had. It can be good or bad.

Most religions believe that God is eternal. That means that, like the Sikh bracelet, God has no beginning and no end. To ask who, or what, made God is meaningless. It is like asking the popular joke question 'How long is a piece of string?'.

Science and religion both accept that some things do not have a beginning nor an end. They are infinite. Science does not look for the centre nor the edge of outer space because space goes on forever. We find it difficult to understand this idea because nothing on earth is like it. Could God be like nothing on earth?

God help you

Family prays for Briton abducted in Indonesia

Miracle baby was answer to woman's prayers

'Thank God she's safe,' says mother of kidnapped Kylie.

Father prays at bedside of dying CJD victim

Many people go through life without giving much thought to religion or to the existence of God. However, when times are stressful, some look to God for help.

Build up a spider diagram with God in the centre. Choose at least eight difficult situations where somebody might turn to God for help. You can use the newspaper headlines to start you off.

God

How do people contact God?

Look at the newspaper headlines and decide how each of the people involved contacted God. Clearly a mobile phone is not going to solve this one.

Prayer

Prayer is likely to be the most common way people encounter God. It does not necessarily involve special body positions. Prayer can be very simple. It can be just thinking of a message in your head. Unlike sending an email, there is no need to even press the Send button. Many religious believers think God knows exactly what is going on inside our heads.

Meditation

Some people feel they can get close to God by just quietly thinking. This is called **meditation**. For some it helps to meditate in the countryside, surrounded by God's creation. Other people prefer pictures or statues to help them meditate. They do not worship these objects; they use them to focus their minds. Christians and Hindus especially find this helpful. Sikhs begin their meditation on God by chanting the words 'Wahe Guru' (meaning wonderful Lord) over and over again.

Holy place – Some people feel the atmosphere of a holy place can help them to feel the presence of God.

Holy books

Many religions feel they make contact with God through the words in their **holy books**. Muslims believe the Qur'an contains words that God gave directly to the Prophet Muhammad. For this reason Muslims say the Qur'an contains God's advice and solutions to all the problems people will ever meet.

Jews also believe their Bible was given to them directly by God. They too turn to it for God's guidance in their everyday lives.

The arts

There are also people who believe they get close to God by doing something physical. This can be dancing, singing, concentrating on painting or perhaps making a sculpture. They lose themselves in the action which frees their mind to be open to God.

- List the ways people contact God.
- Why do Muslims believe the Qur'an particularly helps them get close to God?

Write a different caption to the picture. Explain how a holy building might help a worshipper encounter God.

- Choose one religion and list the different ways followers might make contact with God. You may need to do further research.
- Use a double page in your exercise book to display the various ways a religious believer could feel close to God.

Experiences of God in the past

Holy smoke!

In Jewish scriptures there are many stories of the prophet Moses having contact with God. Moses' first encounter with God was when he was a shepherd out in the desert. On that occasion he saw a bush on fire, but the strange thing was that the bush did not get burnt. It remained the same. Moses heard the voice of God coming from the bush, telling him to lead the Jews out of Egypt to freedom.

Years later Moses heard God's voice on the top of a mountain. There was thunder and lightning, even trumpet blasts. Fire and smoke covered the top of the mountain and the voice of God was heard. On that occasion God gave Moses the laws he wanted the people to live by.

Moses became a great teacher and leader of the Jewish people, making them into one nation.

This stained-glass window shows Saul's experiences.

It happened in a blinding flash!

Cave visions

One famous Christian encounter with God happened to Saul who was terrorising the early Christians. He arrested them, burnt their houses, destroyed their meeting places and even arranged for some to be killed.

While travelling on his way to terrorise yet more Christians, Saul was suddenly blinded by a bright light. The experience terrified him, especially when he heard a voice speaking to him. Saul fell to the ground. He was told to go to the next town and await further instructions. Those who were with him had to help him because he was blinded.

This dramatic experience changed his life. Saul obeyed all the instructions he was given and got his sight back after three days. From then on he was a different person. To show this, he changed his name to Paul and instead of terrorising the Christians, he joined them.

Paul did such important work in spreading Christianity that after his death he was known as Saint Paul.

Muhammad was a wealthy merchant in the town of Makkah in Saudi Arabia. His money had been gained honestly from marriage to a wealthy widow and his own clever trading. Although Muhammad seemed to have everything a person could want, he was dissatisfied. He felt sure there was more to life.

As a young man he was in the habit of leaving the town and going away on his own to meditate. On one occasion as he sat in a cave on the side of Mount Hira, just outside Makkah, he saw a vision of an angel. The angel brought Muhammad words from God, which he memorised. The words were dictated to a scribe. Over a period of 23 years, Muhammad received the contents of a book, the holy Qur'an.

Muhammad was changed by his experiences and went on to teach people how to live in the way God intended.

GOING FORWARD

- Look at page 62. Read about the Sikh leader Guru Nanak's encounter with God.

- Compare all four accounts. List their similarities.

- Do you think experiences like this happened only in the distant past?

- Compare the effect these experiences had on each person. What did they do afterwards as a result?

ACTIVITY A
- Write an account of Saul's experience for the evening paper. Include an interview with him and either somebody who was with him, or one of the Christians he had been torturing. You can get more details in Acts 9:1–19.

- Write a letter from a friend of one of the people mentioned on these pages or on page 62. Comment on what is supposed to have happened to them and how it has changed them. You can be sceptical about it if you like.

Recent encounters with God

Bernadette Soubirous

Bernadette lived in the south of France near the border with Spain. When she was 14 she had an experience which changed her life. She was out collecting firewood for the family with her sister and a friend when she walked by a cave. The other two had gone on ahead. Bernadette heard a breeze and saw the bushes at the cave entrance rustle. Then she saw a light and had a vision of a woman. No one else saw this. It happened on several occasions and the vision spoke to her. Bernadette believed she saw Mary, the mother of Jesus, and that the vision was sent by God. Bernadette's life was changed by her experience.

She decided to become a nun and help sick people. The place where she had the vision, called, Lourdes, has become a centre for pilgrimage and worship. In 1933, some years after her death Bernadette was made a saint by Pope Pius XI.

Today thousands of people travel to Lourdes. Some believe that they too have an encounter with God. For most it does not take the form of lights or a vision of the Virgin Mary. It may just be a sense of closeness to love. A few people have been healed of diseases but for many the healing is spiritual.

Jackie Pullinger

Jackie left England in 1966 when she was 22 years old. Although she had trained as a music teacher, Jackie was sure God really wanted her to teach people about Christianity. Without any clear idea of how to do this, she booked a ticket to Japan. When the boat reached Hong Kong Jackie felt God was telling her to disembark. She couldn't speak any Cantonese or Mandarin, but managed to get a job in a mission school in a very poor area of Kowloon. There she worked among drug addicts and criminal gangs teaching them about Jesus' love and care for the drop-outs in society. She put that love into practice by helping people recover from addiction and start a new life. Even though she had no money, her prayers and trust in God were answered.

Jackie Pullinger has been able to help many young men give up heroin and crime. Money and assistance came from unknown sources to help her set up homes for addicts who lived on the streets but wanted to change. Many have become Christians because of her example. Others have been cured of their drug addiction by praying to God for strength to fight their dependency.

Jackie Pullinger works in the back streets of Hong Kong helping drug addicts and criminals.

Cicely Saunders is the founder of the modern hospice movement in Britain.

Cicely Saunders

In 1947 Cicely Saunders was a medical social worker. At that time she met David who was dying of cancer. For two months Cicely visited him regularly and often talked to him about his death. She became aware how much talking helped David to be less frightened and more comfortable in his final days. It also convinced her that hospitals were not the best places for dying people. However, she did not do anything about her ideas for a while.

She says, 'While reading the verse "Commit thy way unto the Lord, trust also in him; and he shall bring it to pass", I felt God was tapping me on the shoulder and telling me to get on with the work. I then started to plan the hospice and to raise money in the city. I never gave up hope, I knew it would happen.'

The first hospice that opened was St Christopher's in London. This was the beginning of the modern hospice movement.

GOING FORWARD

Read about Mother Theresa's experience of God on page 38.

- Write a series of five imaginary diary entries for one of the women mentioned here, or for Mother Theresa. You need to include something about their everyday work as well as their religious life.

- Write down the different ways these women experienced God and what they did afterwards.

- Make up three questions you would like to ask one of them during a radio phone-in or an on-line chat.

Other modern experiences of God

Dead Man Walking

This is a scene from the film 'Dead Man Walking' which was made about the life of Helen Prejean.

This encounter with God has become famous since a Hollywood film was made in 1994. Helen Prejean was a nun in America who had spent most of her time quietly teaching until she was sent to a housing project in New Orleans in 1981. The area was known for guns, drugs and crime. There with five other nuns she helped run a home for 1500 very poor people. One of her tasks was to teach people writing and to write letters for them. She was asked if she would consider becoming a pen-pal to a person on Death Row. Feeling that God wanted her to do this, Helen agreed.

She wrote to the murderer Elma Patrick Sonnier who had shot and murdered two teenagers. After writing for several months Helen visited him in the notorious Angola Prison in New Orleans. During her following regular visits, Helen Prejean helped Sonnier talk about his crimes. She helped him to accept what he had done and prepare for his death and God's judgement. It was her encouragement that led him to read the Bible. Eventually he told her; 'I am sorry for what I have done. I don't think people can forgive me, but I think God can.'

Sonnier was sentenced to be executed by electric chair when his pleas for a stay of execution were refused. He asked Helen if she would remain with him as he died. This was a tremendous ordeal for her and one she was only able to face after praying to God for strength to help her through.
On 4 April 1984 she watched through a glass panel as Sonnier was electrocuted. His last words to her were to ask the father of the victims to forgive him.

Helen Prejean has continued working with prisoners on death row and with the victims of their crime. She feels that they too need help and support. As a result of her encounter with God in the prison, Helen is convinced that the death penalty is wrong. She is an important campaigner for the abolition of the death penalty.

Encounters with God do not always happen in religious places. Helen Prejean's desperate prayers asking God to give her strength to stay with a murderer during his execution took place in a ladies' toilet next to the cells in Death Row.

Not everybody experiences God in such dramatic ways as the people featured here. For some the experience can be just as profound but quieter. It may not cause them to change their life radically either.

Just to look up into the night sky and see the huge number of stars or to walk in peaceful, beautiful countryside may make some people think there is another force more powerful than us.

LOOKING BACK

- Look back over pages 21–26 and list the many different places people have encountered God.

- Write a press release for the film *Dead Man Walking*.

- With a partner discuss whether you think Helen's work with Sonnier was worthwhile?

- Do you feel she ought to have spent more time with the teenagers' parents than with the murderer?

- What do you think Helen would say?

1 Draw a poster to show the idea of God as the designer of the universe.
2 'Meetings with God only happened in the distant past.' Prepare a short talk about this.
3a Which of the arguments for the existence of God do you find the most believable? Why?
  b Which of the arguments for the existence of God do you disagree with most? Why?
4 Read this quotation and then write the meaning in your own words.

> Whoever it was who searched the heavens with a telescope and found no God, would not have found the human mind if he had searched the brain with a microscope.
>
> G. Santayana, *RE Today*

GOING FORWARD

1a Research more information about Dame Cicely Saunders and the modern hospice movement.
  b Find out what sort of care is provided in a hospice? Can they help babies and young children?
  c Where is the nearest hospice to your home?
2 Consult these websites to find out more about arguments for the existence of God
• www.re-xs.ucsm.ac.uk
• www.theresite.org.uk
3 This picture is the Hindu goddess Lakshmi. Find out what this picture symbolises about Hindu beliefs in god.
4 Choose one person whose life was changed by an encounter with God and plan an assembly round the idea.

What is justice?

That's not fair!

Do you think that 'justice' is the same as 'being fair to another person'? Some say that life is never fair; if you are born in a palace or a slum that will make all the difference to how easy it is to get on in life.

Many people believe that British justice is the best in the world. However, occasionally there are miscarriages of justice, like the case of the Birmingham Six. The picture on the previous page shows the Birmingham Six in 1991, after the Court of Appeal found them not guilty of killing 22 people in a bomb attack on a Birmingham pub in 1974. These six people had been wrongly imprisoned for 17 years.

Read this story.

This statue stands above the Old Bailey, which is the most important court in Britain. The statue symbolises justice. What features can you see? What do you think they have to do with justice?

Steve had very little money and the bills were mounting up. He asked his cousin Sarah, who had recently won a huge amount on the lottery, if he could borrow £100. He said he would pay it back in two weeks when he got paid for his job collecting trolleys at the supermarket. The next day he was dismissed by the supermarket and a fortnight later still did not have the money to pay her back. Sarah was annoyed. 'He shouldn't have asked for the money, if he couldn't pay it back,' she said. 'That's not fair,' and she took him to court.

Her friends were shocked. 'That's tight. She has so much money, she can afford to give him some. Call it a donation to charity,' one of them laughed.

They all went to hear what the judge would say.

'Stephen Perkins must pay back the money he owes,' said the judge. 'That is justice.' Everybody was horrified. They expected him to be more sympathetic. But then the judge reached across his table and picked up a small cardboard box. Looking directly at the people who were listening to the case, he said, 'Now all of you who can help Stephen pay what he owes will be showing kindness.'

> If you were the judge would you have made Steve pay the money back?

- Do you think the law is fixed or should be altered to suit people's circumstances?

- Would you fine a Ferrari driver the same amount of money for driving at 40 miles an hour in a 30 mile-an-hour zone as the person driving a ten-year-old family saloon car?

An eye for an eye and we shall soon all be blind
Mahatma Gandhi

What did Gandhi mean? Do you think it is justice to give back exactly the same as you received?

Read the story of King Solomon judging the case of who is the real mother of a baby. The story is in 1 Kings 3:16–28. Solomon's decision is just but is it kind? It is actually a very clever one. Why do you think so?

What is just?

A woman steals a pack of nappies from the supermarket for her baby. When she is caught she says she cannot afford to buy them. What do you think would be a just punishment?

Two girls steal a 50p piece from the pocket of teenager in a wheelchair who is waiting to cross the road. Should the punishment take into consideration the amount of money or the state of the victim?

Your old pencil case is stolen from your schoolbag. You were going to throw it away that evening. What would be a just punishment for the culprit?

A vigilante group burns down the house of a suspected child abuser. Is that justice?

ACTIVITY A Use the story as the basis of a play. You can develop it further to include what happens outside the courtroom. Either work it out as a role-play or write it as a script.

What do people judge?

In pairs list the sort of things people judge you on. Here are a few ideas to start you off – your clothes, the colour of your skin, where you live, what sort of car you drive, etc. Against each one write down who you think comes off worse in each case.

Racism

Judging a person is inferior to you because they come from a different race is wrong. Christians believe that God created everything, which includes all the people in the world. Is it possible that God would create some people of a lower standing than others? Christianity, indeed all religions, says no. This should mean that every one is entitled to the same treatment. The Bible says God created humans like himself. Therefore, treating some people badly because they look different might be like treating God badly.

Prejudice

There are many areas where people are prejudiced against other people. Prejudice means making a judgement against someone without examining the facts. Some people make unfair judgements based on gender. In the past women have found it difficult to get jobs that truly reflected their ability. This is because it has been said marriage and having children should be the only job women do. Although Christians believe all people are equal, some Christians are having to consider their attitude towards women becoming priests and bishops.

Gender prejudice can also work against men. There has been prejudice against men becoming nurses or helping in nursery or infant schools. They have often been told that it is 'women's work'.

Disabled people also find it difficult to get fair treatment. Firms do not offer them a job in case they are 'a nuisance'. Companies are not always prepared to make the necessary physical alterations to accommodate disabled people.

Would you treat this person in the same way as you treat people you meet at school? Why? Are you being prejudiced?

Wealth and poverty

We cannot help noticing those people who have money and those who do not. There are differences within the school, within our own society and in the world. Some people have lots of money because they have worked for it, but others work just as hard and do not have a fortune. How hard do lottery winners work for their money? Is there any justice here?

We often see scenes of terrible poverty in the developing world on the television. No matter how hard people there struggle, they seem powerless to improve their situation.

As members of one large family created by God, Christians believe it is their duty to care for other members of that family.

Crime and punishment

In many ways this topic is different from the other three. When you think of a judge, it is usually to do with criminals. Most people think we should do something about anti-social behaviour that harms another or damages property. Christians believe that criminals should be punished for their crime. This might cause problems if it means deliberately hurting the criminal. What concerns Christians most is the reason for the punishment. They believe punishment should be designed to reform the criminal rather than just get revenge.

Christians also believe that God gave each of us free will. We can choose how we behave. We can deliberately do something wrong, or choose to do right. Christians believe they should lead the sort of life that God wants. How can any person know what God wants? Christians believe that God sent his son Jesus to earth to show them the correct way to live. Through Jesus' teachings and the way he lived his life, people can see an example of how to live a good life.

Women still find prejudice towards them becoming priests.

What is meant by prejudice?

- Which form of prejudice do you think causes the most trouble in your school at the moment?

- What is being done about it? What else do you think could be done to change attitudes?

Jesus and justice

One of the things that Jesus stressed was that God wants justice in the world. Everybody has a right to be treated fairly. Jesus said that Christians who see injustice happening should do something about it. He did.

In Luke's Gospel (4:18–19) Jesus gave his followers a clearer idea of justice when he spoke of God's intention. Jesus said:

> He has sent me to proclaim liberty to the captives and recovery of sight to the blind; to set free the oppressed and announce that the time has come when the Lord will save his people.

Passages like this have inspired some Christians to fight injustices in their own society.

Christians differ in the ways they believe Jesus intended them to fight injustice. Some say the occasion may demand violent action to destroy evil. Only when that evil is destroyed will peace and justice have a chance. There is one story in the gospels of Jesus throwing over the tables used by the money-changers and tradesmen in the temple. He chased them out saying they were turning the house of prayer into a hideout for thieves (Matthew 21:12–13).

Some argue that Jesus' message was revolutionary because he taught that love would overcome injustice. Jesus told his followers this in Matthew 5:39 and Mathew 10:34–39.

> Do not take revenge on someone who wrongs you. If anyone slaps you on the right cheek, let him slap your left cheek too.

MEEK. MILD. AS IF.
Discover the real Jesus. Church. April 4.

Some Christians think of Jesus as a radical leader who was quite prepared to fight the injustices of his time. He did not promise his followers an easy time either.

> Do not think that I have come to bring peace to the world. No, I did not come to bring peace, but a sword... Whoever does not take up his cross and follow in my steps is not fit to be my disciple. Whoever tries to gain his own life will lose it; but whoever loses his life for my sake will gain it.

As a class discuss whether the pacifist approach to bullying in the playground would work. What other ways are there for defusing a violent situation?

In 1989 the Chinese authorities sent in tanks to break up a peaceful protest in Tiananmen Square in Beijing. A brave student stood in the square as a tank rolled up towards him. It got right in front of the student, then the driver stopped. He could not bring himself to kill an unarmed protester. The whole world saw the success of this peaceful stance on television.

I was hungry and you fed me, thirsty and you gave me a drink; I was a stranger and you received me in your homes, naked and you clothed me; I was sick and you took care of me, in prison and you visited me... I tell you whenever you did this for one of the least important of these brothers of mine you did it for me!

Matthew 25:35–40

Jesus also told his followers it was simple justice to help someone in need. Whoever they helped it would be the same as if they had helped Jesus. God would reward their kindness in heaven.

Re-write the passage above in your own words. If you are able, write it in a modern-day setting.

Does justice have to be harsh?

Jesus showed that it was possible to be just and show forgiveness. Read the story of the lost son in Luke 15:11–32.

- Do you think the father behaved justly towards the younger son?

- Did the father behave justly towards his elder son?

- How was forgiveness shown by the father?

ACTIVITY A

- Role-play a situation where a bully continually threatens someone. When the victim calmly challenges the bully to hit him, the bully cannot do it and is embarrassed.

- Tell the story of a modern family situation where justice and forgiveness are shown.

St Paul and justice

Jesus' words and example have been very important to Christians and so have the words of another Christian teacher, St Paul. He lived after Jesus and they never met each other.

Paul's early life as Saul, the killer of Christians, was mentioned on page 23. After his life-changing experience, Paul worked to spread the words of Jesus around the Roman Empire. The teachings of St Paul are helpful to Christians today because he explained in great detail what Jesus meant. Paul wrote letters to the new Christian communities he helped establish, telling them how to put Jesus' words into practice. Read the different extracts from his letters here and try to work out what Paul says is a just way to behave.

> If someone has done you wrong, do not pay him with a wrong. Try to do what everyone considers to be good. Do everything possible on your part to live in peace with everybody. Never take revenge, my friends, but instead let God's anger do it. … If your enemy is hungry, feed him; if he is thirsty, give him a drink; for by doing this you will make him burn with shame. Do not let evil defeat you; instead conquer evil with good.
>
> *Romans 13:17–21*

A second letter to the Roman community

> Love one another warmly as Christian brothers, and be eager to show respect for one another. Work hard and do not be lazy. Serve the Lord with a heart full of devotion. Let your hope keep you joyful, be patient in your troubles, and pray at all times. Share your belongings with your needy, fellow-Christians, and open your homes to strangers.
>
> *Romans 12:10–14*

Letter to the Roman community

> There is no difference between Jews and gentiles, between slaves and free men, between men and women; you are all one in union with Christ Jesus.
>
> *Galatians 3:28*

Letter to the Galatian community

> **List eight different things Paul tells this Roman community they should do.**

- With a partner, examine what Paul says. Decide whether you think his advice is fair or not. Give a reason for your decision.
- Why do you think Paul tells the new Christians to act in this way? Do you think it would work?

These words were revolutionary at the time. The Jews thought there was a big difference between themselves and the Gentiles, that is, people who did not obey the Jewish rules about food and other things. Christians today believe these words give them guidance on racism. What is the connection?

Another letter to the Galatians

'Love your neighbour as you love yourself.' But if you act like wild animals, hurting and harming each other, then watch out, or you will completely destroy one another.

Galatians 5:14–15

- What does Paul say will happen if you treat someone badly?

- People sometimes say it is 'poetic justice' when a person does something bad to another only to find it rebounds. Write a short story where that happens. Call it 'Serves you right!'

- Find out where Galatia was.

- Read through these quotations from St Paul. Compare them with the words of Jesus on the previous page. Copy into your exercise books one quotation from Jesus and one from St Paul which you think are saying the same thing.

- On a double page in your exercise book, put the title 'Christian justice' in a box in the centre. Display ideas, quotations or images around the box to help someone understand the concept.

Mother Theresa and justice

Becoming a nun

Agnes Bojaxhiu grew up in a Roman Catholic family in Macedonia, in the former Republic of Yugoslavia. From an early age she wanted to become a nun and trained in Ireland, taking the name of her patron saint, Theresa. From Ireland she went to India to teach. Life in India was a shock. There was terrible poverty and people were left to die in the street without care. She said, 'I saw bodies on the streets, stabbed, beaten, lying there in dried blood.'

Mother Theresa founded a home to care for people who had been left to die. She ensured they were looked after lovingly and allowed to die with dignity.

Encounter with God

Travelling on an Indian train one day in 1948, Theresa became aware that God was telling her something. 'The message was quite clear, it was an order. I was to leave the convent. I felt that God wanted something more from me. He wanted me to be poor and to love Him in the distressing disguise of the poorest of the poor,' she said. That was the start.

Mother Theresa learned basic medical skills so she could live among the poor and help them. Other nuns soon joined her and the Missionaries of Charity was founded. Those who chose to join these nuns promised 'to give whole-hearted and free service to the poorest of the poor'. Inspired by Jesus' love for the poor and the outcasts, the nuns went out on to the streets and collected people who had been abandoned to die. They found babies dumped in rubbish bins and lepers whom nobody wanted to touch.

What did Mother Theresa achieve?

For over 40 years Mother Theresa worked to 'do something beautiful for Jesus', as she put it. Some people were inspired by her example and joined her. Today her work has spread way beyond India and men, as well as women, work for the Missionaries of Charity.

- 450 centres have been set up in 100 countries, including Britain
- 90 000 lepers have been treated; at first this was with a mobile leprosy unit travelling to them but later Mother Theresa had a permanent home for lepers built
- 27 000 people who were abandoned to die were able to die with dignity
- 5 000 000 families have been fed
- homes were founded for people with AIDS, alcoholism and drug problems, as well as for abandoned babies and children.

In 1979 Mother Theresa was awarded the Nobel Peace Prize for her work amongst 'the poorest of the poor'. She died in 1997 but her life as a Christian was so exceptional and inspirational that it is thought the Roman Catholic Church will make her a saint in the future.

What did Mother Theresa say about her work?

- 'To fulfil our mission of compassion and love, to the poorest of the poor, we go, seeking out in towns and villages all over the world, even amid squalid surroundings, the poorest, the abandoned, the sick, the infirm, the leprosy patients, the dying, the desperate, the lost, the outcast, taking care of them, rendering help to them, visiting them assiduously, living Christ's love for them, and awakening their response to His great love.'

- 'What these people need even more than food and shelter is to be wanted. They understand that even if they only have a few hours left to live, they are loved.'

- 'Being unwanted is the worst disease any human being can experience.'

Sometimes people were very suspicious about Mother Theresa's work. One Indian official went to take a look himself. He turned up without any warning and was shocked to see her bending over the face of a beggar, picking maggots from the man's wounds with tweezers. After that he never doubted her dedication.

- **Who would Mother Theresa say was not being treated justly?**

- **What did she do about it?**

- Write a press release explaining why the Nobel Peace Prize committee has decided to award Mother Theresa the prize in 1979.

- Write a diary entry for one day, or brief entries for a week, in the life of Mother Theresa. Include quotes from her own words if you wish.

Does justice have anything to do with treating people with dignity. What does that mean anyway?

LOOKING BACK Look at the words of Jesus on pages 34–5. Copy out the passage you think might have inspired Mother Theresa the most.

Desmond Tutu and justice

> Christian worship can never let us be indifferent to the needs of others, to the crisis of the hungry, of the naked and the homeless, of the sick and the prisoner, of the oppressed and the disadvantaged.
>
> Archbishop Desmond Tutu

Compare what Archbishop Desmond Tutu said with Jesus' words in Matthew 25:35–6 and 40 which appear on page 35. What do you think Archbishop Tutu was saying?

Racial injustice

Desmond Tutu was born in South Africa in 1931, during a time of apartheid. Black people were treated as an inferior race to whites. The South African government was white. It forced two million black people out of their homes to create a 'Whites only' area. Black men were sent away from their families to work for very low wages. Their families were left behind in broken-down huts and not allowed to go into white areas, which always had the best facilities. Blacks were often arrested for no reason and imprisoned without trial.

Desmond Tutu trained as a priest in South Africa then went to London University to take his degree in 1962. In Britain he saw a society where blacks and whites lived and worked together without apartheid rules. He returned to South Africa to train black priests and became the first black man to reach high office in the South African church.

Violence

In the black community of Soweto near Johannesburg a violent uprising began. The whites wanted to stop black people using their own language and insisted Afrikaans must be taught in black schools. Having lost almost everything else, black people were determined to keep their language. Trouble flared up and 600 black people were killed.

Peaceful protest

Tutu could not ignore the troubles of his fellow black people. As a Christian he was sure Jesus was on the side of the poor and the oppressed. Tutu argued that the Bible showed God had promised freedom to his people from earliest times when He rescued the slaves in Egypt. Tutu was sure God would help the blacks in their struggle for justice but was equally sure that Jesus' message was one of love. Tutu never supported violence but did everything possible to draw attention to the injustice blacks suffered. He led protest marches and was arrested many times. His powerful, but peaceful, campaign drew admiration from the rest of the world and in 1984 Tutu was awarded the Nobel Peace Prize. But in South Africa nothing changed.

In 1986 Tutu became the first black Archbishop of South Africa and used his new position to draw the world's attention to the way blacks were treated. He led a peaceful march onto a whites-only beach and was beaten off with whips. Tutu also appealed to the world not to buy South African products. This meant the white government lost so much money they were eventually forced to listen to the black people's requests.

Success finally came in 1994 when South Africa held the first elections in which black people were allowed to vote. This led to the election of Nelson Mandela, the first black president of South Africa.

Throughout the long struggle for justice Tutu found strength in Christianity.

> If it were not for faith, I am certain lots of us would have been hate-filled and bitter … But to speak of God, you must speak of your neighbour … He does not tolerate a relationship with himself that excludes your neighbour.

In this peaceful protest Tutu led blacks onto a whites-only beach. Later they were chased off with whips by white police.

- If Archbishop Desmond Tutu was to spend time in Britain today do you think he would say everybody is treated justly and equally?

- Write a newspaper report of Tutu's march on the whites-only beach. Decide whether you are writing for a black newspaper or a white newspaper of the time. Would it make any difference?

- Who do you think Archbishop Tutu would include as a 'neighbour'?

- When Jesus is asked who your neighbour is, he tells the story of The Good Samaritan. Read it in Luke 10:29–37.

ACTIVITY

Design a certificate that might be handed to Archbishop Desmond Tutu with his Nobel Peace Prize. What will it say on it?

Others search for justice

Many people have worked for justice in the past and still do today. Not everyone is necessarily a Christian. The people on these pages share a belief in non-violence.

Read all three accounts.

- List the injustices each man wanted to change.

- What is meant by the term 'civil disobedience'?

In groups, design a poster to illustrate one person's fight for justice. You may need to add some research of your own.

Research the life and work of someone with a completely different approach to justice. Camillo Torres was a Roman Catholic priest who believed in using violence to end violence. He said, 'I believe that the revolutionary struggle is appropriate for the Christian.'

Or

Research the American Muslim black rights leader Malcolm X who also thought it was necessary to fight evil with violence.

Choose one of the people who worked for justice. Write a letter from them to the authorities explaining why people should be treated equally. The letter should include some religious teachings.

The Dalai Lama

The Dalai Lama on the right meets Archbishop Tutu. Both men believe in the power of peace. The Dalai Lama is the leader of the Tibetan Buddhists. He was born in Tibet, a mountainous country often called 'the roof of the world' because it is dominated by the Himalayas. In 1949 China invaded Tibet and many Buddhist monks were beaten up and even killed. The Dalai Lama escaped to India which is his home today. He travels the world campaigning for Tibet to be free from Chinese oppression and for international peace. The Dalai Lama's work earned him the Nobel Peace Prize in 1989. You can also see him on page 100.

Mahatma Gandhi

Many people think of this Indian man as the greatest leader in non-violence of the twentieth century. Gandhi was a Hindu who respected all world religions. On page 31 is one of his famous sayings. He also said that he had read the New Testament, and found Jesus' teachings about peace especially useful. Christians have found great inspiration in Gandhi's ideas and work.

Gandhi was born in India on 1869, studied law in London, then worked in South Africa where he saw the beginning of a campaign to get equal rights for black people. When Gandhi returned to India in 1894 he began to work to get the British rulers out of the country and let Indians govern themselves. Gandhi was convinced that the campaign could only be achieved by peaceful means. His methods included a boycott of everything British. That means he and his supporters would not buy anything made in Britain, or use British schools, courts or offices. This was called civil disobedience and landed him in prison. He went on hunger strike as a way of drawing attention to the plight of some members of the Indian community. Eventually, as a result of Gandhi's non-violent campaign, India gained independence in 1947. Gandhi continued to work to bring calm to the communities but he was shot by a Hindu fanatic as he made his way to evening prayers in January 1948.

Martin Luther King

Martin Luther King was a black Baptist minister who was inspired by Gandhi to change the way black people were treated in America. Black Americans did not have the vote, earned half as much as whites and were not allowed in the same areas as whites. In one famous incident a black woman, who had paid for her ticket on the bus, was told to give up her seat to a white man. When she refused she was arrested. King led a peaceful campaign of civil disobedience. Black Americans refused to travel on the buses so the bus companies, owned by whites, lost lots of money. For over ten years King used marches and speeches, and refused to do certain things, but he never resorted to violence. As a result of his campaign black Americans were given the vote in 1965. Three years later Martin Luther King was shot dead by a white assassin.

In his most famous speech King said 'I have a dream that one day all God's children, blacks, whites, Jews, Gentiles, Protestants and Catholics will be able to join hands and sing in the words of the black people's old song, "Free at last, free at last, thank God Almighty, we are free at last".'

LOOKING BACK

- Look back through the previous pages and list the names of those who were awarded the Nobel Peace prize for their efforts. Find out who won the prize last year?

Other Christian ideas about justice

Prisoners of Conscience

People who have been imprisoned or tortured for their political beliefs are called prisoners of conscience. Many Christians believe this is unjust because people should be free to hold their own opinions. Jesus, too, was a prisoner of conscience. He suffered and died for his beliefs.

Amnesty

One way Christians help is by supporting the charity Amnesty International. This is not specifically a Christian charity; Amnesty International helps people of any religion, colour or race. Amnesty campaigns at international level to get justice for prisoners of conscience. They write letters to the authorities that confine prisoners of conscience. Some Christians support Amnesty's work by letter writing, donating money to the charity and through prayer. In some churches and cathedrals there are special chapels dedicated to prisoners of conscience. Each week or month, worshippers direct their prayers and letters towards helping particular prisoners.

Peter Benenson, founder of Amnesty International, said: The candle burns not for us, but for all those whom we failed to rescue from prison, who were shot on the way to prison, who were tortured, who were kidnapped, who 'disappeared'.

- Look at the logo for Amnesty International and the explanation of it by Peter Benenson. As a class, brainstorm words you think of as you consider this. Use these words to write a short poem.

- Why might a candle be a suitable symbol for Amnesty International?

- How is a candle used in Christian worship?

This candle burns in the Prisoner of Conscience Chapel at Salisbury Cathedral. The candle has many symbolic features. It is based on Amnesty International's logo. The burning candle in the middle reminds Christians of the light of Jesus in prison. The barbed wire represents the crown of thorns that was rammed down on his head before he was crucified. The spikes remind Christians of the nails that pierced Jesus' hands. The sculpture was inspired by the words in John's gospel (1:5): 'The Light shines in the darkness and darkness cannot overcome it.'

Terry Waite

Terry Waite was released after five years in prison in Beirut. As a Christian he had gone to try and arrange for the release of hostages captured in Lebanon. He was captured himself.

Terry Waite was adviser to the Archbishop of Canterbury. As a Christian he believed in justice and, despite the dangers, travelled to talk with foreign governments to try and get hostages freed. In 1981 he successfully negotiated the release of British hostages from Iran and in 1985 got others released from Libya. The following year he agreed to help the Americans try to get US hostages out of Beirut. This time Waite was captured. From January 1987 until November 1991 he spent five years in prison. During his solitary confinement something unexpected happened.

'One day, out of the blue, a guard came with a postcard. It was a postcard showing a stained glass window from Bedford, showing John Bunyan in jail … And I turned the card over and there was a message from someone whom I didn't know, simply saying, 'We remember, we shall not forget. We shall continue to pray for you and to work for all people who are detained around the world.' That thought sent me back to the marvellous work of agencies like Amnesty International and their letter writing campaigns and I would say, never despise those simple actions. Something, somewhere will get through to the people you are concerned about as it got through to me and to my fellows eventually.'

from Terry Waite's homecoming speech

- **What did Jesus tell his followers to do in Matthew 25:35–40 about people in prison (see also pages 34–5)?**

- **How do some Christians put this into practice? Research the work of two Christians groups, the Salvation Army and the Quakers, in prisons today.**

- **Discover more about Amnesty UK's work on their website www.amnesty.org.uk**

ACTIVITY A Cut out some card to make a postcard. What image would you choose to put on the front of a postcard going to a prisoner of conscience that might give them courage? What message would you write on the back to a person you have never met?

Why do some give their lives for others

Monday 24 March 1980

GUNNED DOWN AT HIS OWN ALTAR!

There was shock and outrage this morning at the news that Archbishop Oscar Romero was shot as he celebrated mass. A single shot was fired. Romero fell dead in a pool of blood on the chapel floor of the hospital. No one has yet accepted responsibility for this killing. It is thought the government is behind this latest outrage.

Man of the people

Romero was the hero of the poor in El Salvador. As a Christian he spoke out about the death squads who roamed the countryside. He held protest marches against the government. At public meetings he accused the government of beating up, even killing, people who dared to complain. Many men, women and even children, he said, had simply 'disappeared'.

Outspoken critic

In the sermons he broadcast on the radio, Romero condemned the government as corrupt. He criticised rich landowners for making huge profits while their workers starved to death. Last month he wrote to the President of America telling him that the money and arms America was sending to El Salvador were being used against the poor. 'Since I am Salvadorian and Archbishop of the San Salvador diocese, I have the obligation to work for the reign of faith and justice,' he told the President.

You are killing your brothers

Only yesterday, Romero urged soldiers to stop the massacres. 'You are killing your own brothers,' he told them. … 'In the name of God, in the name of this suffering people whose cry rises to heaven more loudly each day, I implore you, I beg you, I order you: stop the repression.'

Inspired by Jesus

Romero tried to follow in Jesus' footsteps by standing up for what is right. Because Jesus gave his life for others, Romero was prepared to die if necessary. He said Jesus' resurrection gave him courage. Friends said that Romero knew the risks and thought he would probably be murdered. But he said if his death helped to bring justice nearer it would not be wasted. 'If I am killed, I will rise again in the people of El Salvador.' He said, 'Let my blood be a seed of freedom, and a sign that hope will soon be a reality.'

Death threats

Romero admitted receiving death threats. Only last month he stopped other priests going with him. He said it would not be fair to expose them to unnecessary risks.

- Why did the government of El Salvador kill Romero?

- Why did Romero take risks?

- The murder of Romero drew world attention to what was going on in El Salvador. Do you think he was brave, or silly, to be so outspoken?

- How was Romero inspired by Jesus?

You can read details of the UN Truth Commission's investigation into Romero's murder on www.icomm.ca/carecen/page41

Two weeks ago a bomb was found behind the pulpit in his church. The bomb had failed to go off. This time he was not so lucky. His killing has all the hallmarks of the professional assassin. Only one shot was fired.

Bearded gunman

An eyewitness said a red Volkswagen had been parked opposite the hospital chapel for a while. A bearded passenger was seen to raise his gun and fire into the chapel through the car window, then calmly pull away into the traffic. Other witnesses to the shooting are asked to come forward.

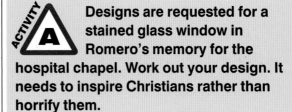

ACTIVITY A Designs are requested for a stained glass window in Romero's memory for the hospital chapel. Work out your design. It needs to inspire Christians rather than horrify them.

How Christian organisations fight for justice

Christian Aid
We believe in life before death

Christian Aid started in 1945 by helping refugees in Europe after the Second World War. Today, it is supported by 40 different Christian church groups in the UK and Ireland and still works with many refugees and people forced to leave their homes. Christian Aid wants everyone, everywhere to have a decent life. It works by helping people to help themselves. It gives money to partner-organisations in poor countries to find ways of helping people to have a better future. Like Jesus, Christian Aid believes in working where it is most needed. It does not matter what a person's religion is. This means that Christian Aid does more than just give poor people money and food. The charity works with local communities to help them sort out their basic problems.

Columbia has been torn apart by battles between different groups for over 40 years. Left-wing guerrillas and right-wing paramilitaries fight each other over land, weapons and drug trafficking. Armed groups try to gain control of the country's rich natural resources – such as timber, emerals, gold and oil. Innocent people are caught in the middle. The fighting groups force these people off their land, either by killing them or making them leave. Over one million Colombians have been forced off their land in the last five years and thousands of people have been brutally murdered.

Most people want to farm and fish peacefully and not get involved in any fighting. In 1997 the people in the community of Cacarica, northern Colombia, were thrown off their land by the paramilitary. They were originally told they had three days to leave and then just three hours! They had to leave behind their crops, their animals, their household belongings and their homes. Many of them only managed to escape with their lives and the clothes on their backs. Some fled to the neighbouring country of Panama; others to the nearest town, Turbo (half a day's journey by boat), where they sought refuge in a sport's hall. In the end, 780 families (3810 people) shared the hall – with no beds, no water, and no pots and pans.

Christian Aid was worked in partnership with the Colombian organisation Justice and Peace in the community of Turbo. They helped to improve living conditions for the people sheltering in the sports hall. However, the people of Cacarica wanted to go back to their homeland. During 1999 and 2000, they returned. With the help of Justice and Peace, the people of Cacarica rebuilt their homes. Justice and Peace also helped the community to develop the principles by which they live their life; these are reflected in the colours of their flag.

> **Yellow represents truth:**
> **Christ died for truth**
> **And for this we are prepared to die.**
> **Red represents freedom:**
> **With truth we feel free.**
> **Blue represents justice:**
> **With truth, freedom and justice**
> **We can build peace.**
> **Green represents solidarity:**
> **Taking decisions together**
> **With all members of the community**
> **Ensures that our project for life will progress.**
> **Brown represents fraternity:**
> **With our indigenous neighbours**
> **And the excluded of the earth**
> **We will join together**
> **To build a world of dignity for all**

- How is Christian Aid putting its message 'We believe in life before death ' into practice in Colombia?
- Read more about Christian Aid's work on www.christian.org.uk

The Catholic Association For Overseas Development has similar aims to Christian Aid. Both believe that Christians have a duty to work for justice. CAFOD says:

> We believe that all human beings have a right to dignity and respect and that the world's resources are a gift to be shared by all men and women, whatever their race, nationality or religion. ... We don't just give money to poor communities and walk away, or just support projects in emergencies. We work hand-in-hand with local people to help them to respond to their own real needs. Come rain or shine, we stick with it. Projects like landmine awareness training, farming skills training and water programmes can take years to complete.

Like Christian Aid many of CAFOD's projects do involve getting emergency food supplies to famine areas, but they also work on other projects. One of these involves getting justice for workers in the clothing trade. Many of the clothes we wear are made abroad. CAFOD believes it is wrong that people should suffer just to make cheap clothes for us.

> We have a factory in China where we have 250 people. We own them; it's our factory. We pay them £23.60 a month and they work 28 days a month. They work from 7 a.m. to 11 p.m. with two breaks for lunch and dinner. They all sleep together, 16 people to a room, stacked on four bunks to a corner. Generally they're young girls that come from the hills.
>
> **Part of an interview with a clothes producer**

More details about the lives of these factory workers and others CAFOD works with can be read on www.cafod.org.uk/garment_industry

> **What do you think the speaker means when he says, 'We own them'?**

> Check through all the clothes you wore at the weekend and list the countries they came from. Would it make any difference to what you bought if you knew how the clothes were produced? Why?

Role-play a television interview between a worker from CAFOD and the factory owner.

- **Why would a Christian organisation like CAFOD want to get involved in the way the Chinese workers are treated?**
- **How do you think these workers are suffering?**

Other ways Christians practise justice

Tear Fund

Every night, across the world, people are going to bed hungry. Every morning millions wake up to a life without proper food, clothing, medical care or education. Every minute 25 children die as a direct result of poverty. Something has gone terribly wrong with our world. While some people feast others starve. Tear Fund believes that this terrible situation is not someone else's problem. It is our problem too. Something can, and must be done.

Fairtrade: guarantees a better deal for Third World Products

Many Christians are concerned that our lifestyle in the West can exploit people in poorer countries. In order for us to enjoy cheap food or clothes, workers in other countries are kept as slaves. Young children particularly are used as cheap workers and kept in appalling conditions. Christian groups like CAFOD and Christian Aid have joined with others to set up The Fairtrade Foundation. They aim to help workers get a fair price for their work and receive just treatment from their employers.

Fairtrade goods are found on many supermarket shelves in Britain and carry the Fairtrade logo. You can buy tea, coffee, cocoa, honey, chocolate and bananas that are Fairtrade.

Tear Fund is a Christian agency that puts Christian love into action by following the example of Jesus. They work all round the world. Read about their latest projects on www.tearfund.org

Their special website for young people is on www.activ1st.org

Did you know?

- The world trade in bananas is worth £5 billion a year.
  - The UK spends £750 million a year on bananas.
    - 95% of British households buy bananas every week.
      - We each eat an average of 12–15 kg of bananas a year.

For every £1 spent on bananas:
- the supermarket gets 32p
  - the grower and pickers get between 3p and 11.5p
    - the rest of the money is taken up by transport, ripening and packing.

'Bananas mean everything in the rural areas. A fair price might mean that, for the first time, farmers could look forward to getting further education for their children. When you buy a cheap banana you are unwittingly participating in the exploitation of labour.'
Windward Island farmer

1 in 5 banana workers in Costa Rica become sterile and women in the packing sheds have double the rate of leukaemia from the use of chemicals. Fairtrade works to reduce the chemicals used in banana production.

ACTIVITY A
- Design a T-shirt that one of these organisations could sell to raise money and which would advertise their work.
- Design a poster to advertise one of Fairtrade's products like tea, coffee, bananas or trainers. More facts can be obtained from www.cafod.org or www.fairtrade.org.uk or from www.ethicaltrade.org

Why do groups like Fairtrade think Christians ought to be involved in their campaign?

It is just and it is fair

- What problem did the cocoa farmers have in Africa?
- On a map, look up exactly where Lameck lives.
- What do you think a co-operative is?

- Why does the Choc Shop claim it is 'A chocolately challenge to bite into poverty!'
- Which Christian organisation is supporting the cocoa farmers?
- How do they claim this is fighting injustice?

You can read more about the launch of 'Divine' chocolate on www.divinechocolate.com

ACTIVITY A
- Design a poster for your school to advertise the Choc Shop. Tell people why they should buy this sort of chocolate rather than their usual one. Tell them where the money your school raises will be going.
- Could you set up a tuck shop to raise money for charity.

Choc Shop

'A chocolatey challenge to bite into poverty!!'

Christian Aid
We believe in life before death

The choc shock!

Chocolate is dee-licious! But it's no fun for people who grow the cocoa beans for very little pay in countries like Ghana and Brazil. Most of them are so poor they have never even tasted chocolate. Christian Aid's sticky-fingered, choc-filled, fun fundraiser – Choc shop – helps you to raise money to help Christian Aid fight injustice and poverty all over the world.

Some sweet ideas

Here are just a few mouth-watering ideas for you to melt together into your own divine creations!

When farmers are paid a fair wage

Find out how fair trade helps Lameck and his family.

Lameck is 12 and lives in Ghana. Until recently he used to helpe on the family cocoa plantation. It was very hard work. Lameck's dad says 'It all changed when we joined the Kuapa Kokoo co-operative which sells cocoa to fair trade organisations.' The Kuapa Kokoo co-operative gives farmers a fair wage for their cocoa beans and is supported by Christian Aid. This means that Lameck's family now has enough money to send him to school. Lameck goes to school most days now and enjoys learning to read and write. He wants to be a doctor.

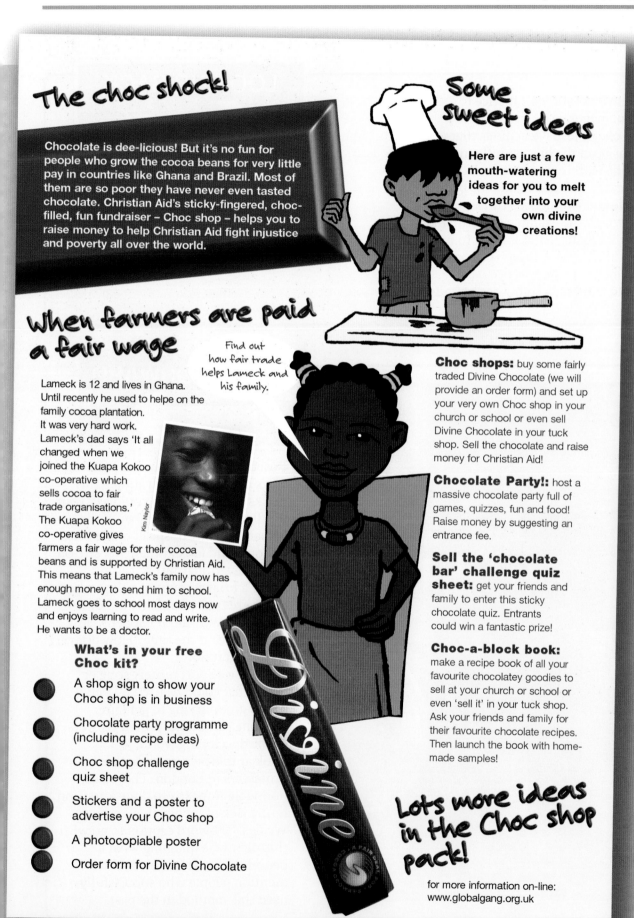

Kim Naylor

What's in your free Choc kit?

- A shop sign to show your Choc shop is in business
- Chocolate party programme (including recipe ideas)
- Choc shop challenge quiz sheet
- Stickers and a poster to advertise your Choc shop
- A photocopiable poster
- Order form for Divine Chocolate

Choc shops: buy some fairly traded Divine Chocolate (we will provide an order form) and set up your very own Choc shop in your church or school or even sell Divine Chocolate in your tuck shop. Sell the chocolate and raise money for Christian Aid!

Chocolate Party!: host a massive chocolate party full of games, quizzes, fun and food! Raise money by suggesting an entrance fee.

Sell the 'chocolate bar' challenge quiz sheet: get your friends and family to enter this sticky chocolate quiz. Entrants could win a fantastic prize!

Choc-a-block book: make a recipe book of all your favourite chocolatey goodies to sell at your church or school or even 'sell it' in your tuck shop. Ask your friends and family for their favourite chocolate recipes. Then launch the book with home-made samples!

Lots more ideas in the Choc shop pack!

for more information on-line:
www.globalgang.org.uk

LOOKING BACK

1 Complete this sentence: Justice to a Christian means ....

2 Choose one of Jesus' teachings that you think has been the biggest influence on Christians working for justice and write it in your exercise book. Name the people who have been influenced by these words.

3 Look through the examples of Christians working for justice. Make a grid to list their names, the different things they have done and the methods they used.
You could work on a computer spreadsheet.

4 Discuss with a partner: Are there any ways in which the Christian idea of justice might be different from the idea of justice in the courts? Pool your ideas for a class discussion.

GOING FORWARD

1 Research details about the practical ways in which the Salvation Army works for justice. You could ask your teacher to invite a member of the Salvation Army to speak to the class, or you could look at their website on www.salvationarmy.org

2 Write a brief account of a time when you were treated unfairly at home or at school. Why did it happen? How did you feel at the time? How do you feel about it now?

3 Compose a short protest song or poem that could be used by a civil rights group trying to get fairer working conditions for tea growers in the developing world.

4 Look at this picture of disabled protesters in London. They used non-violent means to draw attention to the lack of money they receive. Write a 100-word caption to go with this picture, explaining what a peaceful protest is. You could mention people who successfully used this method in the past.

Unit 3 › WHY IS GURU NANAK IMPORTANT TO SIKHS?

Guru Nanak

- What do you think the artist was trying to say about the type of person Nanak was? Compare this painting with the one on the previous page.

- Look at the light around Guru Nanak's head. What could that mean?

- What is his expression? Is it sad, happy, thoughtful, calm, angry, holy or would you say something else?

- What can you say about the way he is holding his hands? Compare this picture of Nanak with those of the Buddha on page 86. Are there any similarities between the two?

- Why do people like to have pictures or photographs of those who are important to them around them?

This is a painting of the Sikh teacher, Nanak. The word 'guru' means teacher, so he is usually referred to as Guru Nanak. No one painted a picture of Guru Nanak in his lifetime, so this is how an artist imagined he would look. As with most great religious leaders, such as the Buddha on page 86, their pictures contain symbolic features.

Nanak born

2000 BCE   1469 CE   2000 CE

Nanak was born in 1469 CE, which makes Sikhism the most recent of the six great world religions.

ACTIVITY A

- Draw a long timeline stretching from 2000 BCE to 2000 CE.

- Write on it the dates when Nanak lived: 1469–1539. Because Guru Nanak is the founder of Sikhism, the date of his birth will approximately mark the beginning of this religion.

Where?

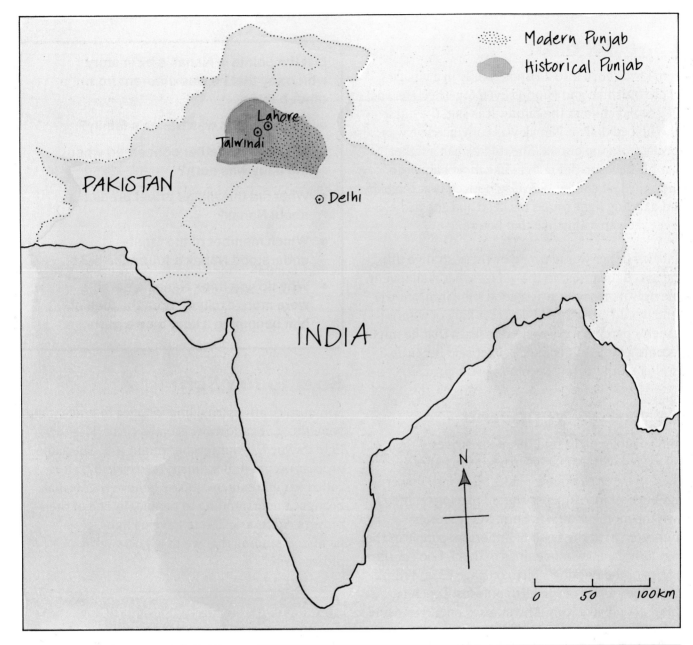

Nanak was born in Talwindi which is now called Nanakana Sahib 'Nanakana' means 'Nanak's village'. 'Sahib' is a term of respect, just as you would call a male teacher 'Sir'. The town was given a new name to honour the great Sikh teacher. Nanakana Sahib is in an area called the Punjab. Today part of the Punjab is in northern India and part in Pakistan.

ACTIVITY A

- Add to your timeline the beginnings of the other world religions, add: 600 BCE for the Buddha; 4 BCE for Jesus; 2000 BCE for Abraham and the beginning of Judaism; 600 CE for Muhammad and the beginning of Islam. Hinduism can only be shown disappearing further back than 2000 BCE because it is the world's oldest religion. It is so old no one is even sure how far back it goes.

- Find out who the king of England was in 1469, when Nanak was born in India, and mark it on the timeline.

A special baby

A special birth

Nanak was born into a Hindu family in a village where Muslims and Hindus lived together. He was the second child in the family. It is said the nurse who helped deliver Nanak was convinced he was special from the outset. She told Nanak's father that his new son did not cry like most babies do. The baby just smiled. She also noticed that the baby had dazzling light round his head and she had never seen anything like that before.

Nanak's father was alarmed by these strange things and asked the priest in the village what it all meant. The holy man said it was a good sign; it meant the child would grow up to be a great king or a guru. Nanak's parents were excited to learn that he might become a king, but Nanak's sister said her little brother would surely become a great guru.

Weird and wonderful

Some people might find the many stories associated with Nanak's birth hard to believe. There are stories of how plants burst into flower and musical instruments started playing on their own the moment he was born. Many stories connected with the birth of important people in the past have strange happenings in them. Look at the stories of the Buddha's birth on page 83 and think about the stories of the birth of Jesus. Legends about people like King Arthur also contain unusual occurrences. Some people believe events like that did happen. Others think ancient story-tellers were using their tales to show the listener that this was the birth of someone extra special.

> **Which would you rather have: the fame of a great ruler or the wisdom of a great teacher? Why?**

> **List the points in Nanak's birth story which say that he was different from other babies.**
> - **What religion was Nanak's family?**
> - **Why was his father concerned when the baby was born?**
> - **What did the village priest predict about Nanak?**
> - **Which member of the family understood Nanak's future life best?**
> - **Why do you think Nanak's parents were more excited about the idea of him becoming a king than a guru**

Seeing the light

Sometimes, after struggling for ages to understand something, it suddenly becomes clear. 'Has the light dawned?' your teacher might ask. The same process occurs in Buddhism (see page 87). It is called 'enlightenment'. Sikhs believe that Nanak brought understanding to people. In one of their prayers, Sikhs ask God to 'give us light, give us understanding that we may know what pleases you.'

> **What could the story-teller and the artist be trying to say about Nanak by using light features in the story and pictures?**

ACTIVITY **A**

- The word 'guru' means 'teacher'. It is actually made from two parts: 'gu' meaning darkness, and 'ru' meaning light. Draw a diagram in your exercise book to illustrate the connection between the idea of light and being a teacher.

- Role-play the conversation between the nurse who delivered baby Nanak and her next-door neighbour later that evening. What is she going to say? What will Nanak's father have told her?

Awkward questions

The Hindu priest gives a sacred thread to the boy as a sign that he has become a scholar.

From stories that have been handed down, the child Nanak must have been like one of those young children who keep asking awkward questions: 'Why do birds fly?' 'Where do babies come from?' 'How big is a star?'

Nanak went to school when he was seven years old and baffled his teacher with his questions. He wanted to know, 'What use is all this knowledge to me?' The teacher patiently explained how it would help him when he was an adult. Nanak asked, 'Will it help me in the after-life?' His teacher did not know how to answer.

Nanak's did not attend school for very long. He would rather sit quietly and think about God than read the textbooks he was asked to read. His parents decided it might be less problematic if Nanak had lessons on his own with a Hindu priest. However, the priest did not find Nanak easy to teach either. As soon as the priest put a sacred thread over Nanak's head, as he normally did when he first taught a pupil, Nanak began asking awkward questions.

'Why are you doing this?'

The priest said it would make him become a good Hindu.

Nanak asked, 'How can a thread make me a good boy? God won't love me if I do bad things, thread or no thread.' The boy went on to ask what the priest thought God was going to do when the thread wore out and fell off.

The priest must have thought his pupil was very clever, especially when Nanak asked why he had to be a Hindu. 'Isn't it better to be a good person?' Nanak asked.

When Nanak was in his teens, his father hoped that his eldest son would join the family business and become a good tradesman. It did not look promising. The young Nanak had a habit of giving away all his property to the poor, including his clothes, his books, and even his shoes. Nanak's father thought that if he trusted his son with an important business task the boy would respond. The father gave Nanak a large amount of money and sent him into the city to trade with it.

On the way Nanak stopped to listen to twenty holy men teach about God. Because these men looked so thin and hungry Nanak spent all the money on food for them. When he returned home he had nothing to show for his visit to the city. His father was furious.

'I have fed twenty starving people,' Nanak told him. 'What could be better work than that?'

'It is through actions that some people come near to God and some wander away,' Guru Nanak said when he was older. In your own words, explain what is meant by this. Which of Nanak's actions do you think show that he was trying to get closer to God?

- People often say that you learn more if you ask questions. Do you agree? Why might asking questions be better than just remembering what you are told?

- List the awkward questions Nanak asked. Could any of those questions have actually taught the listener a lesson, even though they didn't answer them?

- Suggest some answers to the questions Nanak asked in each story?

ACTIVITY A

- Write a paragraph from Nanak's school report. What would the teacher say about him?

- Write a story about a four-year-old who is always asking difficult questions.

Encounter with God

Vanished

Nanak married and had two sons. It was his custom in the morning to get up early and go down to the river to bathe, then say his prayers. He usually returned and went to work. One day in 1496 he didn't return. His friends went down to the river to see what had happened but there was no sign of him. His wife was upset and convinced he had drowned. Only Nanak's sister trusted that he would return. She said he still had a lot of things he wanted to do for people on earth.

Three days later Nanak reappeared in the village. His family were overjoyed. Then they started questioning him: 'Where have you been all this time?'

'Nowhere,' Nanak replied, 'I have been here with God. Now I have lots of work to do for people.'

'There is no Hindu, there is no Muslim.'

Someone asked Nanak if he had work to do with the Hindus or with the Muslims who lived in the village.

'Everybody is equal,' Nanak said. 'We have all been created by God. It does not matter whether we are black or white, male or female. God does not see a Hindu or a Muslim, only his children. There is only one God.'

This was a new way of thinking for Nanak's family, the people in the village and everybody in the country. The Hindus had a fixed caste system which meant that you were born into a certain group and no matter what you did, you stayed in that group all your life. Some people might be born into a high caste with lots of rights. Others might be born into a low caste with very few rights. If you belonged to a low caste you were not likely to get much education or the chance to earn lots of money. People were not allowed to marry out of their caste nor to mix with those from a different caste. Certain jobs were kept for people of certain castes.

Nanak's message that everybody was equal in the eyes of God was revolutionary.

How old was Nanak when he had this encounter with God? Page 56 will help.

Nanak's sister seems to have had a good understanding of her brother. How do we know?

 **LOOKING BACK**

- Look back to the story of Nanak's birth on page 58. How did his sister show her special understanding of him then?

- Nanak said, 'There are no rich, no poor, no black and no white before God. It is your actions that make you good or bad.' Re-write this in your own words.

- Do you think some people could be specially chosen by God to do certain tasks? Why?

- Guru Nanak said he had been with God. Many people today talk about having experiences of feeling God's presence. What makes them think this is what has happened to them?

TALWINDI TIMES

Price **4** rupees

NANAK VANISHES. FOUL PLAY SUSPECTED.

Stop press

Shock re-appearance of Nanak

Write an account of Nanak's disappearance for the local paper. You need to explain who he is.

- Try to interview his wife but, if she is too upset to speak, perhaps interview his father. Include his sister's views.

- You could include suggestions about what might have happened to Nanak.

- You may use the headline here or change it to suit your story.

- You could include a picture of Nanak or of the river bank where he was last seen. Details of his appearance, height, etc. would be helpful. Also tell people who they should contact with information.

- This newspaper also has a Stop Press column. This column is for any late news that arrives as the paper is being printed, such as sports results. News comes in that Nanak has just been found. Include a brief account of this. What did Nanak say to them?

You could use ICT to write this report if you wish. That might enable you to import and include pictures.

Guru Nanak's teachings about God

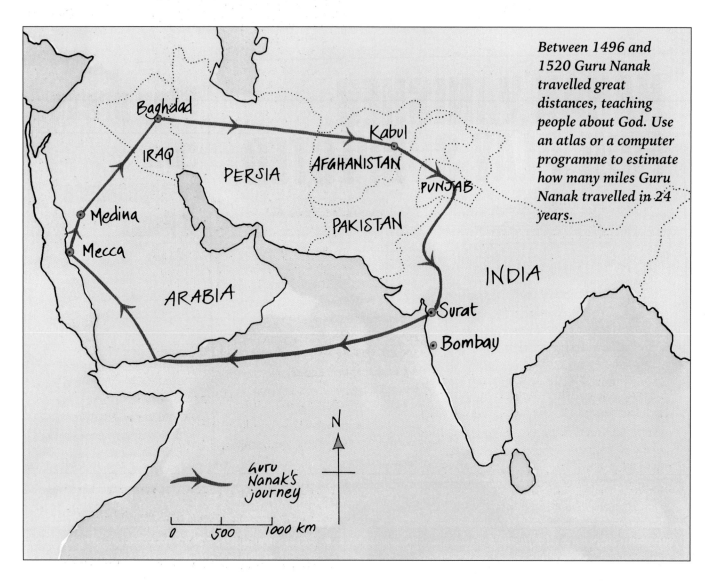

Between 1496 and 1520 Guru Nanak travelled great distances, teaching people about God. Use an atlas or a computer programme to estimate how many miles Guru Nanak travelled in 24 years.

Nanak becomes a guru

After his encounter with God, Nanak knew he must teach others what he had learned. He felt people also needed help in putting God's teachings into practice. What mattered was how you lived your life; it was not enough only to think differently. Nanak left his family in the village and became a travelling teacher. From then on he was known as Guru Nanak.

Guru Nanak taught that God is everywhere. He also taught that God is in everybody, which makes everyone equal. God is neither male or female, so a Sikh would not say 'he' when talking about God. In Christianity we often say 'He' when we refer to God because it sounds rude to say 'it'. Guru Nanak used the words Sat Nam and Waheguru for God. *Sat Nam* means 'the Eternal Reality' or 'the Timeless One', and *Waheguru* means 'wonderful Lord'.

Mool mantar

There is one God

Whose name is Truth,

The creator,

Without fear

Without hate,

Immortal,

Beyond birth and death,

Self-existent.

Made known by grace of the Guru.

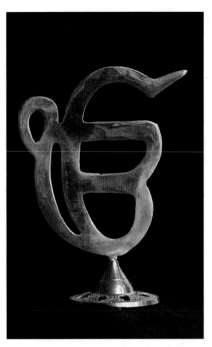

This symbol is called Ik Onkar. It is the first words of the Mool Mantar written in Gurmukhi script. It says 'There is one'. Copy the Ik Onkar into your exercise book. A thick felt pen works best.

This summarises the Sikh belief about God. The words are called the Mool Mantar and were written by Guru Nanak. Because this is such an important statement it is found at the beginning of the Sikh holy book. Sikhs also recite these words every day to remind them of the greatness of God.

- The True One is not far from us, but resides within us.
- God has no form and no features and is revealed only through the True Word.
- To remember God is to live. To forget him is to die.
- Men and women are all equal before God.
- It is through actions that some come near God and some wander away.
- There can be no love of God without active service.

- Look up the word immortal in a dictionary. What was Guru Nanak saying about God when he used this word? How does this idea fit with the name Sat Nam?

Class discussion: 'It is what you do that matters, not what you think.' Would you agree with this? Would it matter if you did something you did not believe in? How much should you be true to yourself? What do you think a monk living in a secluded monastery in the mountains would say to this statement?

ACTIVITY A Read through the selection of quotations from Guru Nanak. Others by him about the environment appear on page 116.

Choose three sayings from the list above to copy into your book. Against each say what you think Nanak meant.

Guru Nanak teaches about equality

On many occasions Guru Nanak said it was not what you believed that mattered as much as what you did. In his teachings and by his example he tried to show people how to lead a better life.

Poor but honest

One story told about Guru Nanak on his travels has a deeper meaning. When Nanak arrived at a village to teach, a poor carpenter called Lalo immediately offered a bed and a meal for the night. Nanak accepted gratefully. Bhago, the richest person in the villager held a huge party that evening to impress people and he invited Nanak as well. Nanak politely refused because he was having supper at Lalo's.

Bhago was offended. 'Why don't you come?' he asked. 'Don't you think I am any better than Lalo?'

'No,' said Nanak.' I don't see any difference between one person and another.'

Bhago was annoyed and insisted that Nanak attend his party. Nanak eventually agreed. When Nanak arrived he carried a piece of bread from Lalo's house in his hand. Just before people began eating Bhago's sumptuous food, Nanak stood up with the piece of Lalo's bread in his hand. Everybody looked up, wondering what he was going to do. The Guru reached for a piece of Bhago's food with his other hand, then squeezed both hands tightly.

From Lalo's bread milk dripped out. From Bhago's food blood dripped out. Bhago was furious at this trick.

Guru Nanak said to him, 'That isn't magic. It is the truth. Lalo may be poor but he has worked hard and honestly to pay for this bread. But you have treated your workers badly. You have squeezed them for every drop of blood in their bodies. That's why this has happened.'

Bhago had no answer. He knew it was true and from then on he treated his workers fairly and with kindness.

Putting equality into practice

Sikhs take Guru Nanak's teachings about equality very seriously. In everyday life Sikhs try to show tolerance. They do not believe Sikhism is the only religion. They understand that it may depend on where you happened to be born as to what religion you follow. Sikhs do not think God belongs to any one religion. All religions offer ways of reaching the same God. What did Nanak himself say about the different religions? Page 62 will remind you.

Women are treated as equal to men in Sikhism, both in the gurdwara (the Sikh temple) and in everyday life. Nanak told his followers to treat women fairly because, 'It is from women that we are conceived and born. Woman is our life-long friend and keeps the race going. Why should we despise her who gives birth to great men?'

- **Bhago learnt two lessons from Guru Nanak. Can you work out what they were?**
- **What reason would Nanak give for treating men and women equally?**

- Re-write the story as a modern one. Who will Bhago become? Maybe he is the wealthy owner of a string of supermarkets where people work long hours for low pay. Lalo might even become one of the check-out staff. Perhaps you have a better idea.
- How do you think Guru Nanak's words, 'There is no Hindu and no Muslim' would affect a Sikh's attitude towards Christians? Why?

This is a painting of the story where Guru Nanak sits down with Lalo and Bhago. Look at the three people in the picture and decide who each one is. What evidence is there to support your decision?

 Draw a series of pictures to show the story of Guru Nanak meeting Lalo and Bhago.

The end of Nanak's life

Nanak travelled hundreds on miles on foot and taught thousands of people for almost 20 years. When he got older he settled down in one place with his wife and family. He taught people at the same time as helping his two sons farm. People who had been impressed by his teachings arrived to live near the great teacher and soon the town of Kartarpur grew up. Its name means 'God's town'.

Nanak knew he must die but that did not frighten him. He was sure that everyone was part of God and would eventually return to God. The soul, he said, lives forever and may be reborn many times before it is reunited with God.

A very wealthy man called Chand wanted to impress people with his wealth, so he went to see if Nanak had an important job for him. Chand was surprised but delighted when Nanak handed him a needle to look after, saying, 'Look after it carefully and please give it back to me in the after-life'.

Chand took the needle home proudly to show his wife. She looked at her well-dressed husband and their beautiful possessions and understood what Nanak was saying. 'If you can't take that needle with you when you die,' she asked her husband, 'how can you take any of your money with you?'

Chand had learned a lesson. He gave his money away and joined Nanak.

Nanak's successor

People thought Nanak's elder son would be their next teacher but Nanak had doubts. When he had asked either son to do a simple job, each had immediately looked around for somebody else to do it. As the Guru's sons they thought they had privileged positions. Often it had been one of Nanak's followers, called Lehna, who volunteered to help Nanak.

Guru Nanak accidentally dropped a coin in a cold muddy ditch. He looked to see if either of his sons would get it for him. Both refused. Without being asked Lehna jumped into the chilly mud, retrieved the money and gave it to Nanak without any fuss. The Guru asked him if he was cold but Lehna said not. He was honoured to serve the Guru and would carry on serving him all his life.

This convinced Guru Nanak that Lehna was the right person to carry on the teaching. Nanak told everyone that Lehna would be his successor and gave him the name Guru Angad because Angad means 'myself'.

- Why would Nanak's sons not have made good Sikh teachers?

- What was the difference between the reasons Lehna and Chand wanted to help Guru Nanak?

- What is meant by a 'global' society? Do you think we have moved towards that today with computers and air travel?

 ACTIVITY A Role-play the scene between Chand and his wife. Show how she helped him understand the meaning of Nanak's task.

- What is reincarnation? Would you say Guru Nanak believed in reincarnation or not? What evidence can you find?

- Discuss with a partner what Guru Nanak meant when he said,'The dead keep their link with the living through the memory of their good deeds.' Do you think that is likely? How long would it last?

Nanak today

Guru Nanak aimed at a global humane society ... He pronounced his universal message loud and clear; all human beings are equal; all have been created by the same God; they are, therefore, sons and daughters of the same creator; it does not matter whether they are Hindus, Muslims, Jews or Christians; they are brothers and sisters. It was a divine and universal message of hope for all of mankind.

Khalsa: The Saint Soldier by S S Narang

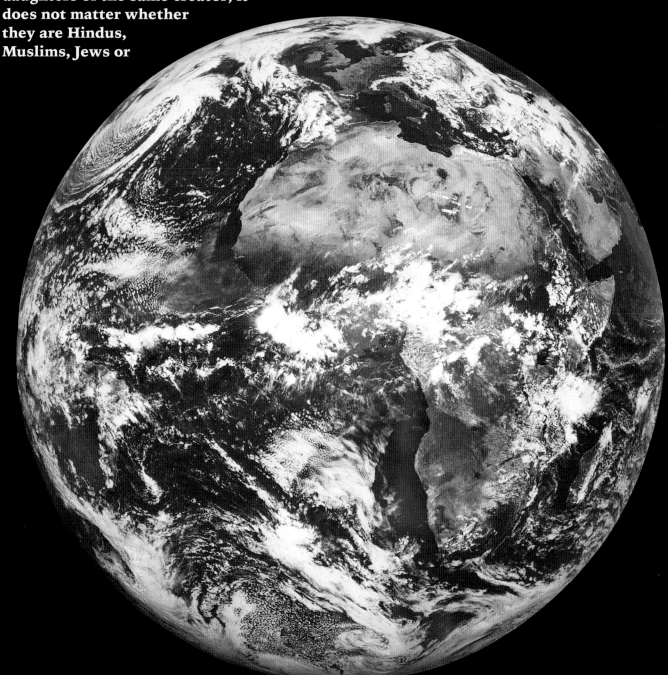

The other Gurus

There were ten human gurus in Sikhism. Before each one died he named his successor. Even the eight-year-old Guru sent his followers to a certain village to find the next guru. The tenth guru, Gobind Singh, said that he would be the last human guru. In future Sikhs would find all the guidance they needed in the holy book. For this reason the holy book is called Guru Granth Sahib. 'Guru' means teacher, 'granth' means 'large book' and 'sahib' is a word that shows respect.

2nd Guru Angad (1504–52)

Angad had been a close follower of Guru Nanak for nine years before he became guru in 1539. Angad was an educated man who wrote poetry and also collected Nanak's words and hymns. Another of Angad's important contributions was devising the Gurmukhi script that is used for writing Punjabi today.

3rd Guru Amar Das (1479–1574)

Amar Das became guru in 1552. He is best remembered for organising the Sikh people into a community. He also spread the message of Sikhism more widely.

4th Guru Ram Das (1534–1581)

This guru founded the holy city of Amritsar. Ram Das became guru in 1574 and is also remembered for many hymns he wrote that are in the Guru Granth Sahib.

5th Guru Arjan (1563–1606)

Guru Arjan was the son of the 4th guru who continued his father's building at Amritsar. Arjan became guru in 1581. He was responsible for building the beautiful Golden Temple at the heart of Amritsar and for gathering the hymns that previous gurus had composed.

This poster shows all ten Sikh gurus and the holy scriptures. Can you recognise Nanak? Why do you think he appears in that position on the poster? Most gurus taught for many years but there is one in the picture who died from small-pox when he was only eight years old. Can you identify him?

6th Guru Hargobind (1595–1644)

By the time Hargobind became guru in 1606, war had broken out in the area. He is remembered for his military triumphs and for the way he trained Sikhs to fight for what is right.

7th Guru Har Rai (1630–61)

Har Rai became guru in 1644. His years as guru were also dominated by war, but Har Rai was concerned to help people who were ill. He set up places where free medicine could be dispensed.

ਉਰੈ ਉਪਮਾ ਤਾ ਕੀ ਕੀਜੈ ਜਾ ਕਾ ਅੰਤੁ ਨ ਪਾਇਆ।।

ਸਰਬ ਜੀਆ ਮਹਿ ਏਕੋ ਜਾਣੈ ਤਾ ਹਉਮੈ ਕਹੈ ਨ ਕੋਈ।।

8th Guru Har Krishan (1656–64)

Har Krishan became guru in 1661. He is the youngest guru and barely had time to achieve very much.

9th Guru Tegh Bahadur (1621–75)

Tegh Bahadur became guru in 1664. This guru was determined to fight for people's freedom to worship in their own way, even though he was arrested and tortured to death. Sikhs remember Tegh Bahadur for his bravery and willingness to die for his beliefs.

10th Guru Gobind Singh (1666–1708)

After Guru Nanak, Gobind Singh was the most influential human guru. He became guru in 1675 and founded the brotherhood of Sikhs. He taught the group how they should live, gave them special clothes and the five symbolic items known as the Five Ks. Guru Gobind Singh was responsible for ensuring the Guru Granth Sahib had a special place in the Sikh faith.

- Why might you find a book on a picture of the Sikh gurus?
- List the advantages you think there might be in having a book, rather than a human, as the teacher. List the problems it might cause.

Copy some of the Gurmukhi script into your exercise book. What makes this writing unusual is that it hangs down from the line above, rather than standing on the line as English script does.

ACTIVITY A Research the Five Ks. Make a poster displaying what each is and why it is important to Sikhs.

- What can you discover about the Golden Temple at Amritsar? Make a leaflet from a folded sheet of A4 paper about this holy place which explains why and how it is important for Sikhs.

Equality in worship

All are welcome

Sikhs make great efforts to put Guru Nanak's teachings into practice. 'We are all God's own people, neither high nor low nor in-between,' he said. Everybody who visits a Sikh temple, or gurdwara, is treated the same no matter who they are. All are welcome to worship in the prayer hall if they wish and everyone is offered food. Many homeless people are grateful to visit a gurdwara where they are treated with respect and given a good meal.

The seating

People who attend the gurdwara for worship sit together on the carpeted floor. Men sit on one side of the hall and women on the other, which is traditional in Indian society. No sex or age group is superior. Rich people sit on the floor alongside poor people; everyone is equal in the gurdwara. The only item of greater worth is the Guru Granth Sahib, which is shown respect by being placed on a cushion, called a maji, and a raised platform, called a takht.

Worship

There are no priests in Sikhism because everyone is equal before God. The person who reads from the holy book is called a granthi and leads the worship. Women as well as men can be granthis, and assist in the organisation and running of the gurdwara. At the end of the service someone distributes holy food to all. The food, called kara parshad, is a sweet mixture of semolina, butter and sugar that has been blessed. A man or woman distributes this holy food to all.

Sharing food

Cooking and eating may seem an unlikely part of worship but Guru Nanak taught that sharing food is a sign of equality and service to others. Gurdwaras always contain a kitchen and dining room and meals are cooked daily. Everyone is offered free meals in the dining room, not only worshippers at the gurdwara. Both men and women donate food, and both share in its preparation and cooking as well as serving it. Children are also welcome to help.

Sharing food and hospitality is an important part of Sikh worship.

- Why don't Sikhs have priests?
- Give the meaning of each of the following words: gurdwara; granthi; kara parshad.
- Why does everybody sit on the floor in the gurdwara?

Does believing in equality mean you should treat everyone the same or does it sometimes involve treating people differently?
Explain your answer by giving examples.

ACTIVITY A

Make a poster of the ways Sikhs show equality in worship. Include these words of Guru Nanak's on it: 'Religion consists not in mere talk. He who looks on all alike and considers all to be equal is acclaimed as truly religious.'

LOOKING BACK

Look back through the story of Guru Nanak and Lalo on page 66. What relevance does it have to the way Sikhs behave in the gurdwara?

Celebrating the life of Guru Nanak

Sikhs enjoy celebrating their own birthdays and those of the gurus. Because Guru Nanak has such a significant place in the religion, his birthday is celebrated by all Sikhs. The festivities can often last three days. In Britain most of the celebration will be on a Sunday because that is the day when it is easiest for people to get time off work and school.

A Sikh festival which celebrates the birth, or death of a guru, is called a gurpurb. The word comes from 'guru' meaning 'teacher' and 'purb' meaning 'holy day'. We might also say holiday.

At the gurdwara

Plans for the celebration of Guru Nanak's birthday are made well ahead. In the gurdwara they centre on a continuous reading of the holy book, Guru Granth Sahib. People come into the gurdwara and listen to portions of it. It takes 48 hours to read the book aloud from beginning to end. Great concentration is required for this and so several granthis are required. Each will read for two hours at a time and then another will take over. The reading begins well before the gurpurb and is timed to finish on the actual morning of the birthday.

Talks about the life and teachings of Guru Nanak will also be given at the gurdwara on the day, special prayers said, and hymns he wrote will be sung.

The street processions are colourful, happy events.

In the street

In areas with a large Sikh population, the streets are decorated with banners hung from lampposts and people spend weeks beforehand decorating floats for the procession. This is led by five men dressed in the traditional clothes that the tenth guru gave his followers. There may be lots of floats and bands in the procession but the main attraction is always the largest float which carries the Guru Granth Sahib. As this processes up the road, a granthi sits on board reading aloud from the holy book. Many Sikhs walk alongside the float quietly singing hymns written by Guru Nanak.

Along the route Sikhs hand out little gifts of sweets, fruit or cooked samosas to anyone who is passing. This is their way of serving others as Guru Nanak taught. Some celebrations end with a big firework display in the evening.

- What is the name for a Sikh festival like Guru Nanak's birthday?

- List the special things Sikhs do in the gurdwara to remember Guru Nanak's birthday.

- Which would be the largest float in the street procession?

- What do people do to show they are trying to keep alive Guru Nanak's teachings about equality?

- It is thought that Nanak was born in April but his gurpurb is traditionally celebrated in another month. Find out which one.

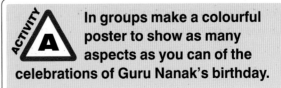

ACTIVITY A In groups make a colourful poster to show as many aspects as you can of the celebrations of Guru Nanak's birthday.

The music of Guru Nanak

Guru Nanak was an educated man who enjoyed music. He wrote down the words and poetry of various people he met on his travels and some of these writings are contained in the Guru Granth Sahib. This is an unusual holy book because it has writings by Muslims and Hindus as well as Sikhs. Guru Nanak had learned from his encounter with God that everyone is equal in God's eyes. He put this into practice by including writings from other religions when he felt they were helpful.

In addition to these writings Guru Nanak is believed to have written 974 hymns that appear in the holy book. In fact, Guru Arjan wrote over 2000 hymns. Nanak discovered people listened and remembered words better if they were put to music, so his teachings were written in the form of poetry. These he sang to an accompaniment played by his Muslim friend Mardana. Religious poetry that is set to music is usually called a hymn.

Guru Nanak's contributions to the Guru Granth Sahib may not be the largest number but they are widely used. The Mool Mantra which appears on page 65 is the opening passage in the holy book. Another of his hymns, known as the Japji, is usually the first a Sikh recites in the morning.

These are extracts from some of Guru Nanak's hymns. Because they are in translation, they no longer read like poetry:

Nanak is shown preaching in this picture. On the left is Mardana, his Muslim friend, who plays the rebeck. This stringed instrument was a present from Nanak's sister to help the Guru's message reach more people.

I was a minstrel out of work.
I became attached to divine service.
The Almighty One commissioned me,
"Night and day sing my praise."
The master summoned the minstrel
To the High Court, and robed me with
the clothes of honour,
To sing God's praises. Since then God's
name has become the comfort of my
life.

Without thee, O my Lord, I know not any other. I ever sing thy praises.

Beyond this earth, there are numberless earths and skies
Rivers and earth innumerable, who can describe these creations?
His lamps are the Sun and the Moon, and His light pervades everything.
If I had a hundred thousand tongues instead of one,
And the hundred thousand multiplied twentyfold,
A hundred thousand times, would I say, and say again,
The Lord of all the people is ONE.

Music forms an important part of Sikh worship in the gurdwara. It is customary for a group of musicians to sit at the front to one side of the Guru Granth Sahib. The musicians are called ragi and may include women or men. Traditional instruments are a baja, which is a small keyboard instrument like a harmonium, and a tabla, which is a drum. Musicians sing as well as play instruments.

- Why would Guru Nanak want to include writings from other religions?

- Choose one of the extracts from Guru Nanak's hymns that seems meaningful to you. Rewrite it in your own words and explain why the quotation you chose seems important and meaningful to you.

- Why did Guru Nanak put his teachings to music?

- What sort of writings did Guru Nanak put in the Guru Granth Sahib?

ACTIVITY
A

Write a brief notice to go on the board at the gurdwara advertising for new members of the ragi.

1   If Guru Nanak had needed a passport for his travels what would have appeared on the application form? You need to include date of birth, birthplace, occupation. You could use ICT to produce this or draw it up on a double page in your exercise book.

2   Write an obituary of Guru Nanak. An obituary is an account of someone's life and main achievements that appears in a newspaper or magazine after their death.

3   In class, discuss which parts of Guru Nanak's teachings, if any, would be the most useful in today's world.

4   In pairs design a questionnaire to find out whether people think equality has been achieved in our society. You can use ICT for this if you wish.

GOING FORWARD

1   Make a poster that includes information about all ten gurus. You will probably need to do further research.

2   Guru Gobind Singh founded a brotherhood of Sikhs. The first group consisted of five men whom he called the Panj Piare. Research the story of their founding and draw a series of boxes to illustrate this story.

There are several Sikh websites you could access for extra information:
www.sikhs.org
www.sikhnet.com
www.sikhseek.com
www.bbc.co.uk/religion/sikhism
www.elite.net/~gurpal/gurus

3   What do you think are the benefits and challenges of wearing clothes that mark you out as different from others? Would 5Ks cause Sikhs difficulties in today's society?

WHO WAS GOTAMA BUDDHA?

How would you describe the landscape in the background? What animals are in it? Does it look a fertile landscape or a barren one?

This statue, and the one on the previous page, are both statues of the Buddha but they look different. The one on page 79 is a modern British statue while this one is an older Indian statue. List the similarities between the two. Look at the eyes, ears, head, hands and legs. All of these features have a meaning. The Buddha himself probably did not look like this at all; each feature is symbolic.

- Research the meaning of the features that you have listed for the statues. The information on pages 82 and 86 will help you.

- Find out what country is shown in the picture. Page 82 will help you. To see if your guess about the animals in the landscape was correct, look at page 89.

This table contains offerings. List as many items as you can identify. Nobody expects the statue to do anything with these items, especially not eat the food! Buddhists show respect for the memory of the Buddha by putting the objects in front of the statue. It is similar to how, and why, some people might put flowers on a grave. They are showing that they care about the person who has died, but certainly do not expect the body in the grave to admire the flowers.

 ACTIVITY A In your exercise book write the heading 'Shrine Offerings'. Draw and label a candle, flowers and incense. Find out what each represents in Buddhism.

Who was the Buddha?

Was he real?

The Buddha was a real person; he was human, not a god. He was born in northern India around 560 BCE and he died 483 BCE. Buddha was not his real name; it is a title. Buddha means 'enlightened one', that is, somebody who has understood ideas that are usually difficult to understand. The Buddha's first name was Siddharta and his family name was Gotama.

Because the Buddha lived more than two-and-a-half thousand years ago, facts about his life are scarce. A few historical details are known and many stories have been passed on. No pictures of him survive. All the statues and pictures we have today are made up and so they will look different. The pictures and the stories often contain features which have meaning. The Buddha's long ears are to show he came from a royal family, who could afford heavy gold earrings. The bump on the top of his head is to show he had special understanding, or enlightenment.

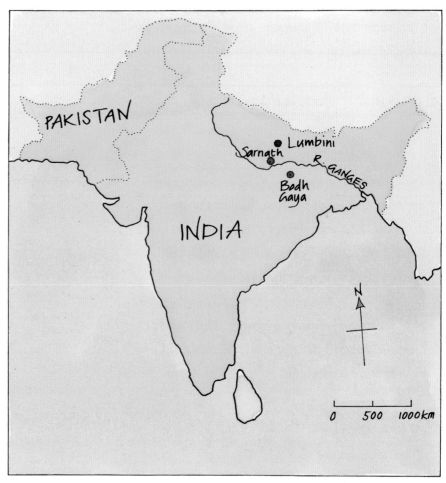

- Why do the dates 560 BCE and 483 BCE appear to be back-to-front in the text?

- As a reporter for the Court News you have been asked to cover the birth of Prince Siddharta. You can use ICT or design a newspaper page in your exercise book. Select six key points from the notes on the opposite page to include in your story. Use an illustration if you wish.

- Which elements in the story do you think might have become exaggerated as the story was passed on?

- Most Buddhists accept this is a story. They believe it was told to show this man was special. List the points you think were meant to show that Buddha was different from other babies.

- With a partner decide what the word 'prophecy' means. Do either of you think such things could come true? How often do you read your stars in a magazine or newspaper? Are they ever accurate?

Once upon a time…

Queen Maya had a dream that a white elephant went into her side. White elephants are rare and a symbol of greatness. Ten months later the queen gave birth to a son.

Strange birth

At full moon in May, Queen Maya was travelling through woodland in Lumbini Park. Suddenly she knew her baby was about to arrive. She reached up to grasp the bough of a tree and the child stepped out from her side without any pain. The baby, Siddharta, immediately took seven steps and spoke. He said this would be his last re-birth and everywhere his foot touched, lotus plants burst into flower.

The prophecy

Later at the palace, Asita, a holy man, called to see the baby. Asita made a prophecy that this child would either grow up to be a powerful ruler or he would become a great religious teacher. The king decided not to leave things to chance; he wanted to make sure Siddharta would rule the kingdom. From then on the king deliberately shielded his son from normal life where ordinary people suffered pain and misfortune. Instead Siddharta spent all his time in the three royal palaces. There was a palace for the winter, one for the summer and one for the rainy season. All had huge beautiful gardens so Siddharta never considered going anywhere else.

To be continued…

Gotama leaves home

Does lots of money bring happiness? Name five ways in which your life would be better with a million pounds. Think of five problems which would be caused by this money. What birthday present could you give a millionaire?

ACTIVITY A

- In groups look through newspapers and cut out any stories involving suffering. They can range from a world disaster to someone whose cat has gone missing. Sort them into incidents where you think somebody was to blame for what happened and those you decide were a complete accident. Use some of the stories, or their headlines, to make a poster entitled 'Why do bad things happen?'

- Design a short questionnaire to record people's views on why bad things happen in the world. You could offer them a choice of reasons, or let them tell you their own ideas. A computer spreadsheet is a good way to present this data.

- In your exercise book write your own captions for the two photographs on this page.

Why do you think this person lives like this? Did he choose this way of life deliberately? Is he happy? Do you think he is suffering? Who is to blame for these circumstances? Should anybody do anything about him?

Life's a party!

Siddharta grew up in luxurious surroundings, spending all his time in the palaces. He had many friends who were all young, beautiful and great fun. It never crossed his mind to go out into the town. Everything he could ever want was available to him. When he was 16, his father even provided him with a wife, a beautiful girl, who produced a son for him.

Life was a continuous round of parties but Siddharta was bored. He felt that there must be more to life than his circumstances, and he asked his charioteer, Channa, to take him into the town. The king immediately ordered all old people and beggars off the streets so his son would not see anything unpleasant.

A glimpse of reality

Despite his father's preparations, Siddharta spotted an old man shuffling along the road.

'What's that?' he asked his charioteer.

'Only an old man, my Lord,' Channa replied.

Siddharta looked confused. All the men he knew were young and handsome. Channa explained that the old man had been fit and healthy once, but like everybody else he grew old and feeble. Siddharta was shocked. He had no idea this could happen.

Later Siddharta saw a man covered in sores slumped down in a corner. Siddharta was horrified and turned to his charioteer.

'My Lord, the man is ill. He can't help it.' Channa explained how everybody falls ill at some time. This was new to Siddharta; he had never seen anyone ill at the palace.

Then a funeral procession passed through the street carrying a corpse. Siddharta stared in horror; he did not know what a corpse was. Channa told him that this was a dead body, adding, 'Without exception, everything that is born will die.'

The prince fell silent. He was shocked to learn that even a king would grow old, fall ill and die.

Further along Siddharta saw a holy man walking along looking content even though he owned nothing and was dressed in rags. This image impressed him. Siddharta's rich lifestyle gave him no pleasure now that he had discovered that nothing lasts forever. He could no longer carry on partying as though nothing had happened. He renounced it all. Home and family were left behind and he went off in search of answers. Why do people suffer? Is there an end to suffering?

To be continued…

Enlightenment

These statues show Siddharta when he became the Buddha. He has a halo round his head and a bump on his head to show he is enlightened. In his hand is a lotus flower and he sits on a lotus throne. The lotus flower is a symbol of purity and enlightenment.

Three Universal Truths

When the Buddha was meditating he became aware of three things. He was certain they were true. They are called universal because it is said they apply to everything in existence.

- Suffering is normal. You cannot escape it. Everybody has their off-days, gets ill and upset about things. You would not be human if you did not suffer.

- Nothing lasts forever. Happy moments and sad ones do pass eventually. Plants and animals live and die. Even rocks are eroded into sand and then into dust. Nothing is permanent.

- Our bodies are always changing. We are not the same people that we were last year, last week, even ten minutes ago. Cells have changed and so have our thoughts. The Buddha decided that no part of a person lasts forever, people do not have a permanent soul.

> With a partner work out if you can think of anything that lasts forever. Do you think the Buddha's Three Universal Truths are true, or not?

 ACTIVITY A

- Draw a diagram in your exercise book to display the Three Universal Truths.

- In pairs role-play an interview for television news with someone who watched the Buddha's enlightenment happen as it is described on page 87.

This shows the Buddha at the moment he became enlightened. It is said he stretched one hand down to touch the earth as a witness to his enlightenment. List the other symbolic features you recognise in this picture.

The wanderer

Once Siddharta was out of the town, he stopped. He cut off his long hair, took off his rich clothes and jewellery and gave them all to Channa to take back to the palace. This showed that he had given up his old life of luxury. He put on basic clothes and walked alone into the forest to join five wandering holy men. For six years Siddharta stayed with them, trying to find the answers to his questions. He ate the minimum to stay alive and became so thin that he could feel his backbone when he touched his stomach. He was in that very weak state when a young female goatherd saw him and offered him ricemilk to drink. Siddharta took it. He decided that pushing his body to the limits of endurance was useless. He was no closer to discovering the meaning of life than when he lived in the luxurious palace. Instead, Siddharta decided he would lead a life between these two extremes.

Meditation

Siddharta sat down under a tree at Bodh Gaya to meditate. As he was quietly thinking, Mara the Evil One appeared and sent various distractions into Siddharta's head to try and make him give up. Tempting visions and horrific images flashed through his mind but Siddharta ignored them. He sat there day and night. Eventually he was ready and his right hand stretched down to touch the earth asking it to witness that he had reached enlightenment.

The enlightenment

At last Siddharta understood everything. This is called the enlightenment. From then on he was called the Buddha, the enlightened one. His understanding gave him great peace and he wanted to pass on to others the meaning of life that he had discovered. Siddharta knew that all things are related to each other. Whatever we do is caused by something and it will have an effect on other things.

To be continued…

The rest of the Buddha's life

The symbol of Buddhism is a wheel which has no beginning and no end. It rolls on forever. The Buddha's teachings are called the Dhamma and often shown as a wheel. The Dhamma had no beginning because the Buddha did not invent the ideas; they were always there. All the Buddha did was to set the wheel in motion by teaching the Dhamma to others. They in turn taught others and so the wheel rolls on without end.

Discuss with a partner: What is your idea of a wise person? Do you imagine someone old or wearing glasses? Would you expect a wise person to be male or female? Is being wise the same as being clever? Have you ever met anyone who is really clever but has no common sense? If you had a real problem with somebody you could not get on with, would you seek help from a wise person or a clever one? Have you ever met anyone you would say was wise?

Wisdom

This is what the Buddha said:

- A fool who thinks that he is a fool is for that very reason a wise man. The fool who thinks that he is wise is called a fool indeed.

- A great rock is not disturbed by the wind; the mind of a wise man is not disturbed by either honour or abuse.

- Rust grows from iron and destroys it; so evil grows from the mind of a person and destroys him.

 Look back over the previous pages giving the Buddha's life story. Write his CV. You can word process this if you wish.

Choose one of the Buddha's sayings to write in your own words or make up a short story to explain the saying.

The life and teachings of the Buddha

The first people who listened to the Buddha were the five holy men he had originally met. It was in a deer park at Sarneth that the Buddha first explained things. His teachings are called the Dhamma. This talk is said to be the first turn of the wheel of the Dhamma. The wheel continued turning because the five men went off and told other people, who told others and so the Dhamma spread.

Some people who listened to the Buddha wanted to live near him so they could learn more. This was the beginning of the first Buddhist community. They were all men. Later, women came to listen to his teachings and asked to join the community. It is said that the Buddha's aunt and his wife were amongst the women who wanted to join. The Buddha thought that the men would distract the women in their search for truth and so he suggested they form separate communities. Today there are Buddhist monasteries for men and separate ones for women.

The Buddha himself travelled around India for 45 years, teaching people what he had learned. By the time he was 80, he knew his life was coming to an end. It is said that he lay on his side under some trees one evening and, after saying goodbye to his followers, began meditating. During the night he meditated into death.

Although the Buddha's followers had asked many times who would teach them after his death, he never named anyone. It is the Dhamma, the Buddha's teachings, which succeed him and the Dhamma continues on over two-and-a-half thousand years later.

The Buddha's teachings today

When the Buddha first talked to his followers in the Deer Park he told them there were four important things to remember.

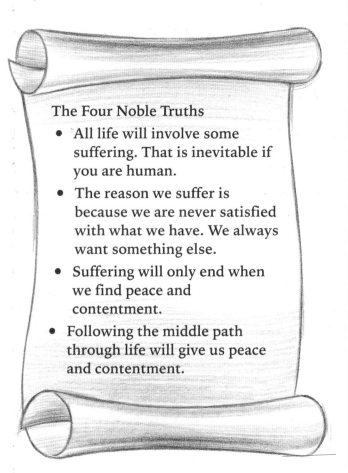

The Four Noble Truths

- All life will involve some suffering. That is inevitable if you are human.

- The reason we suffer is because we are never satisfied with what we have. We always want something else.

- Suffering will only end when we find peace and contentment.

- Following the middle path through life will give us peace and contentment.

This couple is very rich. With your partner, decide whether you think they are content. Will they ever have worries in the future? Does money put an end to suffering?

- Read through each of the Four Noble Truths. Try and work out what they mean. Then share your views with the class on whether you think there is any truth in them.

- What is a craving? Could the Second Noble Truth perhaps be linked to a craving? Could it be the key to unhappiness? Do you think a lottery winner would ever be discontent with life?

 Look at the photograph of Mother Theresa on pages 38–9. She owned nothing but two sets of clothes – one to wear and one in the wash. Many would say she was content.

When people asked for further advice about how they could live a contented life, the Buddha suggested these guidelines. They are called the Five Precepts.

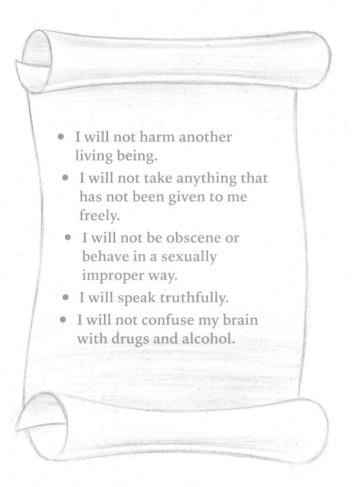

- I will not harm another living being.
- I will not take anything that has not been given to me freely.
- I will not be obscene or behave in a sexually improper way.
- I will speak truthfully.
- I will not confuse my brain with drugs and alcohol.

The Five Precepts are guidance for everyday living. They are not called rules because the Buddha accepted that people might break them. Buddhists try to live by the Precepts. For those who wanted to become monks and live like the Buddha himself, he added a further five precepts, which are on page 96.

Look up the Ten Commandments in Exodus 20. Draw a column down the centre of a page in your exercise book. Label one column the Ten Commandments and the other, the Five Precepts.

- **Write the Five Precepts in its correct column, leaving two lines between each one.**
- **In its own column, match the Ten Commandments against the Precepts. The balance of the Commandments should be written underneath in its column.**

In pairs read the following cases and decide how Buddhists would behave if they follow the Five Precepts. Share your conclusions with the rest of the class. Be prepared to defend your decision with some good reasons.

- A girl picks up a £10 note on the classroom floor after the form has gone out. What should she do?
- A boy is offered drugs at a party. What would he say?
- A boy is told a dirty joke that is really funny. Should he listen carefully then entertain his friends with it?
- Gossip is being passed round the form, which a girl knows is not completely true. How will she react?
- Make up one more situation that you can ask the class.

 Role-play or write a script where a 'poor little rich girl or boy' who has everything is dissatisfied.

The Noble Eightfold path

The Buddha was asked for more details about following the middle path. He gave his followers a list of eight points for guidance rather than rules. This is called the Eightfold path. The path can lead a person through their life. Some people like to think of the eight points as spokes on a wheel and if you look at the wheel of the Dhamma on page 88, you can see why.

- **This path is also called 'the middle path'. What were the two extremes of living that Buddha tried out himself?**

- **Notice that each of these steps say you should 'try'. The Buddha was human and knew it was difficult to obey the rules. These are guidelines how a person could behave. Do you think this is helpful?**

- **Which of the eight steps would you find the most difficult to follow?**

- **Choose three steps and give an everyday example of what a Buddhist could do to follow them.**

Would pupils respond better to school rules if they were guidelines or would nobody take any notice of them?

The staircase is coloured in different bands because each colour involves a different behaviour.

The lower band is called 'the way of wisdom'. Look back to what the Buddha said about wisdom on page 88. Do these steps tie in with it in any way? It might be easier to call these steps 'a way of thinking'.

The middle band is about how you behave.
- Think of three jobs that would be unsuitable for a Buddhist because those jobs harm life.
- Think of three jobs that a Buddhist would consider as 'right livelihood'.

The highest band has ways of training the mind to think. Many people would say they are the most difficult.

Step Four – Right action

Try to do things you know are correct. A Buddhist would use the Five Precepts to help them. These are shown on page 91.

Step Three – Right speech

Try to tell the truth and not get involved in lies or gossip.

Step Two – Right attitude

Try to think positive thoughts which means thinking kind thoughts about people rather than finding fault.

Step One – Right understanding

Try to see things as they really are. You should accept that nothing lasts forever.

Step Eight – Right concentration

Try using meditation to reach a higher level of understanding. Details of meditation are on page 94.

Step Seven – Right awareness/ mindfulness

Try to be fully aware of what is going on in yourself and in others.

Step Six – Right effort

Try to think about what you say and do before acting.

Step Five – Right livelihood

Try to choose a job that does not destroy any life or hurt anything or anyone.

This tranquil pool is in the garden of a Buddhist Centre. Which step of the Noble eightfold path would it best help?

Meditation

Meditation is a term for quiet thinking. Many of us often do that at some point in the day. The difference between ordinary thinking and meditation is that meditation calms the body as well as the mind. It is a way of relaxing. Buddhists believe that once the body is relaxed it is easier to work towards spiritual development.

Why meditate

We lead busy lives, dashing from place to place and getting very stressed. Taking time out to meditate can be deeply relaxing. It is like re-charging the batteries. When you give yourself time to think calmly, you often find a solution to a problem that has been bothering you for a while.

No one told the Buddha the answers to the questions that had been bothering him. The answers were inside him all the time. He just needed calm to find them.

By trying to bring their minds under control, Buddhists believe they can push negative thoughts away. They have space then for feelings of kindness and generosity towards others, helping them reach enlightenment like the Buddha.

DIY guide to meditation

Trying the Buddhist meditation in the classroom is difficult. You may be tempted to giggle. You would need the same power Siddhartha found to ignore the distractions of Mara. However, once you have worked out what you have to do, try to meditate at home.

Sitting

People say it helps to sit upright with a straight back. Hands are rested loosely on your lap, right hand cupped in left. Look back at the pictures of the Buddha and see how he is sitting. It is easier with your eyes shut or, like the Buddha, you can look down to avoid being distracted.

Compare this exaggerated idea of meditation with the photograph opposite.

Thinking

It is difficult to think of nothing when someone tells you to. Thoughts pass through your mind like a troop of monkeys swinging through the branches; no sooner has one passed when another follows closely behind. It helps meditation if you have something on which to focus your thoughts. Some people like to imagine a scene. It might be a smooth lake where a pebble has been dropped and the ripples are gently flowing outwards. Others stare into a candle flame and concentrate on it.

Breathing

Concentrating on your breathing is another way of calming the mind and the body. As you breathe in count steadily to four, then breathe out more slowly to a count of eight. Do several of these slowly. They quieten you down.

Meditation is not easy; it takes lots of practice. You may want to start with meditating for ten minutes at first, then increase the time. With lots of practice a Buddhist can meditate for an hour or more.

Write a magazine article on meditation. Explain how Buddhists use it. Also tell readers why they might find meditation helpful for relieving stress.

No one sees us but ourselves

No one can and no one may

We ourselves must walk the path

The Buddha shows the way.

Buddhism teaches that all the answers are inside. Meditation helps people reach the answers.

The life of a modern Buddhist monk

Are all Buddhists monks?

Only a few Buddhists choose to be monks; most live and work in the ordinary world. Traditionally only men over the age of 20 can become monks because they have had time to live in the world and decide for themselves if they really want this lifestyle. In some countries where there are not many schools, boys enter monasteries for a few years to receive an education. There is no facility for girls to receive a similar education, even though some Buddhist groups allow women to become monks and run their own monasteries. (They are often called monks rather than nuns.)

A person who enters a Buddhist monastery gives away all his ordinary possessions and receives simple robes. It takes about two years of study before new entrants are ready to become full monks. The head monk asks them various questions to make sure they understand the sort of lifestyle they are adopting.

The monk's precepts

A Buddhist who decides to become a monk will already be living by the Five Precepts. For a monk the third Precept about not getting involved in sexual misbehaviour is interpreted as not having sex at all. Buddhist monks believe sexual behaviour will distract from their search for enlightenment. Monks also follow five additional precepts making up Ten Precepts. The extra precepts are:

- to avoid eating after midday
- to avoid entertainment
- to avoid wearing perfume and jewellery
- to avoid sleeping on a deep, comfortable bed
- to avoid handling money.

As a sign that a monk has become part of the monastery, his head is shaved and the white robes he wore as a novice (or learner) are changed for the colour that the monastery wears. It could be dark red, black or saffron yellow.

By shaving his head, wearing plain clothes and following a simple lifestyle, a Buddhist monk copies the way the Buddha lived.

Typical daily life of a Buddhist monk in Thailand

4.30 a.m.	wake-up bell so the monk can wash and dress in robes	Rest of morning	monks have to clean up their living area, wash their robes, then spend rest of morning studying Buddhist teachings.
5.00 a.m.	morning chanting with other monks followed by meditation	11.00 a.m.	main meal of the day which must be finished before noon; no food can be eaten again until sunrise the next day
6.00 a.m.	walk into the villages to receive gifts of food from the local people then carry food back to the monastery	Afternoon	working, studying or meditation
7.00 a.m.	food is shared out; everyone eats breakfast	7.00 p.m.	evening chanting and group meditation
		11.00 a.m.	go to bed.

A Buddhist monk in Britain would follow a similar routine and probably teach aspects of Buddhism in the afternoon or evening. He would not go out to collect food. Supporters of the monastery bring food to the monks and others come to cook it for them.

- Use the timetable as the basis of a monk's diary. Further research would enable you to add more details. There are website references you could try on page 102.

- www.concentration.org gives more details of the Thai monastery and useful help on meditation.

Write a magazine article about life in a Buddhist monastery.

Draw two columns in your book. On one side list the things a monk does when he enters the monastery. On the other side write the equivalent things the Buddha did in his life.

ACTIVITY A Make a poster for the entrance to a Buddhist monastery, displaying the precepts a monk should keep.

Life with a modern Buddhist group

These Buddhists live and work in a women's group called Taraloka. Their community is in the Shropshire countryside. They do not call themselves monks or nuns because their lifestyle is not the same as those of monks in monasteries.

Not all Buddhist groups in the West wear robes. Neither do they all try to lead the same life as the Buddha led in India 2500 years ago.

The Friends of the Western Buddhist Order were founded in 1967 and have adapted the main teachings of the Buddha to modern life. At the heart of this group lies the Western Buddhist Order whose members are ordained Buddhists but wear ordinary clothes. They wear a white or gold sash around their neck when they are teaching. Some live in a single-sex community; others live in the outside world with their families.

The Buddhist women in the picture above organised a retreat centre for women. A retreat centre is a place where people can go to escape from the pressures of daily routines. Here they join with others and use meditation to achieve calm. Women, some Buddhist, many not, can spend a weekend or a week learning meditation techniques or studying the Buddha's teachings. The Order members who run the retreat look after their visitors and teach them about the middle path.

The retreat centre is run on Buddhist principles and the food provided is vegetarian.

These Buddhists in Manchester believe that by helping people they are putting the Buddha's teachings about kindness and care for all living beings into practice. What type of food do you think they serve in their café? Why? The Manchester Buddhist Centre is also involved in education, producing school textbooks about Buddhism and other resources to use in the classroom. This is also a 'right livelihood'. In the picture some Buddhists teach a yoga class.

- **Compare these pictures with the one on the previous page. Discuss the differences with a partner.**

- **Why do you think these particular Buddhists choose not to eat meat? The answer lies in the first Five Precepts on page 91.**

The centre in Manchester is very different from Taraloka but organised by the same type of Buddhists. It is in the heart of a bustling city and many people visit it every day. A group of Buddhist men live and work here but many other Buddhists, both men and women, work at the centre and live elsewhere. The Manchester Buddhist Centre presents courses that help to keep the mind and body healthy. Courses on yoga, acupuncture, homeopathy and pain management are taught at the centre. Buddhists believe that if you have a healthy body it helps you have a healthy mind and both assist people in their search for enlightenment. Most people who attend the courses are not Buddhists but still think the courses are useful to them.

In pairs discuss:
- Could the body have any effect on the mind?
- Could the mind have any effect on the body?

- **Find information on acupuncture, yoga and homeopathy. Write a sentence about each one so that people will know the difference between them. Some are called 'alternative medicines'. What are they an alternative to?**

- **Both Buddhist centres on this spread are putting 'right livelihood' into practice. Look back to page 93 to remind yourself what 'right livelihood' is. Why would their jobs be called that?**

ACTIVITY A

Design an A5 poster that Taraloka or the Manchester Buddhist Centre could display about themselves.

The lay Buddhist's life

This person is a lay Buddhist. He helps to support the monks who live at this monastery by showing school parties round. Here he demonstrates how robes are tied.

What is a lay person?

A person who follows the teachings of a religion, but does not become a priest or a monk, is called a lay person. There are always many more lay people in a religion than priests or teachers. Some people may be lay Buddhists because their parents were and they were brought up that way. Others might choose to become Buddhists when they are older because they think it is the best way of life for them. Several well-known American stars have been interested in Buddhism at different times,

The Hollywood actor Richard Gere, who has become a Buddhist, meets the Dalai Lama, a great Buddhist leader. Read more about the Dalai Lama on page 42.

like Tina Turner and Madonna. The actor Richard Gere took his interest further and has become a Buddhist.

Andrew's story

Andrew is not a media star; he is just an ordinary person who is a lay Buddhist. He lives with his wife and children in Birmingham and works in an office in the city. Andrew became interested in Buddhism as a student. After reading about the Buddha's teachings, he visited one of the many Buddhist communities in the city. Talking to the monks and listening to their teachings helped him sort out his ideas. He went to weekly meditation classes and eventually decided to become a Buddhist. Everyone is welcome to attend events at the Buddhist monastery, whether they practise a religion or not.

Andrew wondered about becoming a monk for a short time. It is possible to follow the Ten Precepts and enter the monastery as a Buddhist monk for just a few weeks, months or years. No life promises are necessary. Some men choose to go into the monastery for a short time because they think the disciplined way of life will help their spiritual development. Andrew decided not to do this.

As a lay Buddhist, Andrew gives some money towards the upkeep of the building but mainly he gives of his time. Other local Buddhist families also donate money but most of it comes from Buddhists who live elsewhere in the country and abroad. Buddhists who live nearby take turns to cook for the monks at the monastery. Others invite the monks to share a meal in their home.

The local lay Buddhists also show school parties round the monastery, clean the building and assist in its running. Andrew monitors the business affairs of the monastery by making sure electric, gas and telephone bills are paid on time out of the donations. At festival times the lay Buddhists buy new robes which they present to the monks, then join together in the celebrations afterwards.

Andrew likes to help the monastic community because he thinks it makes him a better person. He believes he is spreading kindness around which makes the world a better place and helps him towards enlightenment.

The monks, in turn, help the lay people by explaining the Buddha's teachings. The monks chant scriptures and blessings, which is believed to spread goodwill into the world.

Although Andrew's wife has not become a Buddhist, she agrees with the idea of showing loving kindness towards all beings. Their children have been brought up to understand many of the Five Precepts. The whole family attends the monastery at festival times, taking flowers to put on the shrine and joining the celebrations.

What time of day would a family have to eat if they planned to share their meal with the monks? Look back to page 91 and check the extra Five Precepts a monk follows on page 96.

- **What does it mean if someone is a 'lay Buddhist'?**

- **Name two things a lay person could do for the monks?**

- **How many Precepts does a lay Buddhist try to keep?**

ACTIVITY A

Fold an A4 sheet to make a leaflet. Use the information contained within this unit on Buddhism to write a leaflet that could be given to schoolchildren who visit the Birmingham monastery Andrew attends. In it you will need to explain:

- **what Buddhism is**

- **who lives in a monastery**

- **what the monks do**

- **what lay Buddhists do for the monks and why they want to do this.**

LOOKING BACK

1 Write sentences to explain what happened in the Buddha's life at each of the places marked on the map on page 82.

2 What else was happening in the world at the time the Buddha was alive? Look to see what was happening in Egypt, Britain, Greece and India in 500 and 400 BCE.

3 Write a short story called 'The middle way is best'. The story should involve someone who makes a choice between two extremes.

4 Re-write the early life of the Buddha in a modern setting. What will the rich pampered son see that makes him think again?

5 Write an answer to this letter in a magazine (use no more than 250 words).

'Dear Editor, I am thinking about becoming a Buddhist monk, but I am not sure if I could stick it for life. What should I do?'

GOING FORWARD

1 Research what Buddhists today do when they visit one of the places associated with the life of the Buddha?

2 Find out where the nearest Buddhist community is to your school. See if it is possible to arrange for someone to come and visit the class to explain about their life.

3 Choose one of these websites for information on Buddhism you could use to make a leaflet:

www.bbc.co.uk/religion/buddhism
www.theresite.org.uk
www.re-xs.ucsm.ac.uk
www.theravada.net
www.buddhanet.net

Unit 5 > What are we doing to the environment?

"This isn't Civilisation is it?"

'GM monkey's fingernails glow in the dark!'

The state of the environment

Only when the last tree has died and the last river has been poisoned and the last fish has been caught will we realise that we cannot eat money.

These words were spoken as long ago as 1855 by a native American, Chief Seattle. What did he mean?

- Study the pictures on page 103 and the one above.

- Write down what is going on in each picture.

- What is the reason for it? (The genetically modified monkey can be used to test cures for human diseases.)

Facts and figures
Did you know?

- We would need the resources of five-and-a-half earths to keep the world's population going if everyone had the same lifestyle as we do in the West.

- Every year half a million people in the world are poisoned by pesticides.

- One long-haul flight uses the same amount of fuel as a small car does in a year.

- There are more than 30 types of whales and dolphins in British waters, yet they have virtually no protection.

- In this age of computers and the internet, we use more paper than ever – a third of a tonne per person every year.

- 10 000 people a year die in the UK as a result of air pollution.

- Tropical rain forests cover 7 per cent of the planet but contain over half the world's species of plants, animals, insects, etc. At the present rate of destruction, they will all be gone in 50 years.

- Every person in the UK throws away four times their own body weight in rubbish per year.

- 2 million seabirds die every year from getting tangled in waste plastic or from eating it.

- 6 million electrical items are thrown away each year in the UK.

- Over the last 30 years songbirds in the UK have declined: song thrushes by 73 per cent, bullfinches by 76 per cent, lapwings by 62 per cent, skylarks by 58 per cent and swallows by 43 per cent.

Will the results of each picture on page 103 be good or bad for humanity? Does it matter to you?

- Should we have complete freedom to do as we like? Look at the story on page 112. Are there any problems with this attitude?

- Look at the Facts and Figures above. Which do you think poses the greatest threat to life on earth?

 ACTIVITY A

- It has been said that we treat the earth like a giant supermarket. Those with enough money grab what they like. Draw a cartoon to illustrate this statement. How do you feel about that idea?

- Choose one problem on the notepad above to investigate further. Find out if anything is being done to solve the problem.

Doom and gloom?

This is one of the posters demanding that lead be removed from petrol.

Followers of the different world religions believe that they have a duty to care for the planet and atheists and agnostics also think the environment matters. They say our survival depends on the survival of the planet.

What can one person do?

We often feel powerless when faced with such a huge global problem. It may seem that one person's ideas do not make much difference but some environmental problems have been changed by individual actions.

The campaign to get rid of lead in petrol started off with a few people's concern about the poisonous gases we inhale. By the 1980s their concern had grown into a national issue. The government was forced to listen and take action. Now unleaded petrol is the normal petrol to use and the air we breathe has improved.

Another public campaign got rid of CFCs, chemicals that escape into the atmosphere and make a hole in the ozone layer. The sun's harmful rays get through and global warming results. CFCs were present in most aerosol cans we used and in fridges, but today are rarely found.

We cannot help but make an impression on the planet as we walk over it. Should that impression be a shallow one, like a footprint in wet sand that vanishes when the tide comes in? Or is it like dynamite blasting a hole in rock. How deep an impression do you think your life makes on the earth? Visit the website www.lead.org/leadnet/footprint to measure your personal ecological footprint on the planet.

Draw a poster to encourage people to take notice of one of the problems on page 105.

OR

Choose an issue that you care about. Tell people what the problem is. Then tell them what they can do about it.

Design a title page in your exercise book entitled 'Give our world a chance'. This will be the opening page for the work you are going to do on the environment. Try using images on your cover page that show what humans are doing to the air, water and land (plant or animal life).

Your school is planning a Green Day. It is going to be called 'Give our world a chance' day. You have been asked to produce the leaflet to be given out to parents, pupils and the media. Part of the leaflet will include information about one world religion or Humanism. Find out what they think about the environment and put it in your leaflet. You will need to say what practical things the religion is doing to help the planet. You can work in a group if you wish then every person can work on a different religion. The leaflet also needs to give advice on what people can do to help.

ACTIVITY

A Find out about any other environmental issues that have been changed by public pressure. You could investigate animal welfare.

What Christians think about the environment

Christians believe people are God's most important creation, which puts them above animals. What does this imply for the way they treat animals?

Creation

Day 1 God made the earth out of nothing. It was covered in darkness and water.

Day 2 God made the sky above the earth.

Day 3 God made land appear from the water and plants grew.

Day 4 God put the sun, moon and stars in the sky. Day and night began.

Day 5 God created birds in the air and fish in the seas.

Day 6 God created animals. Then God created people both men and women.

Day 7 God rested because creation was complete.

This story on the left was probably being told four thousand years ago, long before there was any scientific evidence. If the story said 24 000 years instead of 24 hours for each stage, would that be more believable? There is at least one entry that does not work scientifically in the order given. Use your knowledge of biology to spot it!

Not all Christians believe the story word for word, but most think it contains the essential truth that everything in existence was deliberately created by God.

The Christian and Jewish creation stories are the same and can be read in Genesis 1.

Stewardship

The Genesis story says: 'I am putting you in charge of the fish, the birds, and all the wild animals.' Christians think this means human life is more important than animal life but humans have a duty to look after animals. Christians believe that people can use the planet's resources for their needs. The Bible also says: 'God looked at everything he had made and he was very pleased.' For Christians this means the planet's real owner is God and we should never do anything to destroy God's creation. Humans only live on the earth for a short time, like caretakers, or stewards, then they hand it back to its real owner in good condition. This is called stewardship.

- **How do Christians think the planet started?**

- **What would they say is the most important part of creation?**

- **What does Christian stewardship mean?**

- **The Orthodox Christians say we should give up some things for the sake of the planet. What could people sensibly give up that would make a difference to the planet?**

- **Read the quotations. Choose one and explain its meaning to your partner. Do you agree with it?**

We do not own the world and its riches are not ours to dispose of at will. Show a loving consideration for all creatures, and seek to maintain the beauty and variety of the world. Work to ensure that our increasing power over nature is used responsibly, with reverence for life. Rejoice in the splendour of God's continuing creation.

Quaker Faith and Practice

The ecological destruction is a form of selfishness arising from the harmful use of creatures, whose laws and natural order are violated.

Pope John Paul II

Christians believe that the world was created by God and continues to be sustained by God. Humans have been given responsibility to care for the world and look after it in a way that safeguards it for the future.

Church of England

Just as a shepherd will in times of greatest hazard, lay down his life for his flock, so human beings may need to forego part of their wants and needs in order that the survival of the natural world can be assured. This is a new situation – a new challenge.

Orthodox Church

ACTIVITY A

Design an Earth jigsaw. Each piece has to build up to a view of what Christians think about the planet. You could research the views of other groups of Christians or include information about creation.

What Christians do for the environment

CHRISTIAN ECOLOGY LINK

'GREEN' SHOPPING...

A responsibility for Christians?

Shopping is fun for many people, a popular leisure activity. For others shopping is hard work. Money, time and energy are limited. To turn shopping into a moral problem may seem to be the last straw!

As you fill your shopping bag, or push your supermarket trolley, do you make time to think about the impact of your purchasing decisions on other people and the rest of God's creation? Do you bring your love for God and God's Earth into your shopping basket?

Everyday actions and decisions **are** important if our Christian faith is to influence our lives. This leaflet has ideas to help connect shopping with Christian discipleship.

How does the Christian Ecology Link suggest people can help the planet?

You can find out more about the work of the Christian Ecology Link on www.christian-ecology.org.uk

> Write a piece for the local newspaper about the environmental work of one Christian organisation. It needs a punchy headline and no more than 300 words of text.

A ROCHA

Christians in Conservation

A Rocha is an international conservation organisation that works to show God's love for all creation in a practical way. This group of Christians started in Britain in 1983 and their first project was to establish a field study centre and bird observatory in Portugal. There they recorded and ringed 50 000 birds and made detailed studies of plants and insects. It was the Portuguese word for 'the rock' – *a rocha* – which gave them their name.

A Rocha has expanded into other parts of the world where they believe conservation and education is badly needed. Here are a few of their current projects:

Kenya – A Rocha, other wildlife groups and churches are working to preserve endangered habitats.

Lebanon – A Rocha are working with local groups to preserve the country's last inland wetland, an important area for migrating waders and wildfowl. They are also studying bird migration patterns.

France – French church groups have joined A Rocha to set up a study centre for research, conservation and education in the Vallée des Baux near Arles.

Britain – A Rocha established a nature reserve on derelict land in Southall, London. In this urban environment they have attracted 80 species of birds and 20 species of butterflies as well as dragonflies and small mammals. Children from all ethnic groups and religions visit the site and take part in activities.

Look at A Rocha's website www.arocha.org to discover more details about the progress of their projects above and read about their work in Canada and the Czech Republic.

> 'Christians believe that God made the world. When we make something, whether it be as life-changing as giving birth, or as quick as sketching a picture, we care about what happens to our creation. So it's easy for us to understand that God cares deeply about all his creation. The Bible makes this clear in many passages, e.g. Psalm 50, verses 10 and 11, where God says "every animal of the forest is mine, and the cattle on a thousand hills. I know every bird in the mountains and the creatures of the field are mine." Studying, thankfully enjoying and caring for the world that God has so wonderfully made is an obvious way for us to show our love for him.'

This is one of the reasons A Rocha gives for Christians being involved in conservation work.

These other websites give details of the practical way in which Christians are helping the environment.

www.church-of-england.org

www.envirolink.org

www.cafod.org.uk

www.cofe.anglican.org

www.christian-aid.org.uk

Christian Aid have a group called Global Gang who are concerned with environmental projects. Read about them on their website above or write for more details with an SAE to: Christian Aid, Global Gang, PO Box 100, London SE1 7RT.

- **Why does A Rocha think Christians should get involved in the environment?**

- **A Rocha believes educating people to care about the environment is just as important as doing conservation work. How do they combine the two? What would be the use of educating people?**

 ACTIVITY A Design a logo for a new group called Green Christians. Your logo needs to symbolise the religion as well as its environmental concern.

Jews and the environment

The world and all that is in it belong to the Lord; the earth and all who live on it are his.

Psalm 24

Look at My creations! See how beautiful and perfect they are! For your sake I created them all. Do not desolate and corrupt My world, for if you corrupt it there is no one to set it right after you.

Jewish scriptures

The rebirth of nature day after day, is God's gift; but humans are responsible for making sure that this rebirth can occur.

Jewish Declaration on Nature

The Earth we have been given is beautiful, bounteous and nourishing to the soul. It was perfectly clean when we got it, and we have a duty to return it to our children in this way.

Clive Margolis

Creation

The Jewish Creation story says God made the universe, the earth and all its life-forms in six days. The story in Genesis 2 is about the Garden of Eden. God created Adam, the first man, and Eve, the first woman, and 'The Lord God placed the man in the Garden of Eden to cultivate it and guard it'. This makes gardening the first job in Jewish history. Jews say it shows God wanted people to work the soil. The animals and birds God created were brought to Adam to be given names which, Jews think, shows that humans are responsible for animal life on earth.

Two men are sitting in a boat out at sea. Suddenly one of them begins to saw a hole in the bottom of the boat. The other man is horrified. 'Hey! Stop that!' he screams. 'What do you think you are doing?' 'Mind your own business,' his mate replies. 'It's my seat. I'll cut a hole under it if I want to.'

What happens next? This Jewish story is saying something about the way we treat the planet. Can you work out what the message is? Read the quotations above which carry the same message. Which one is closest in meaning to the story?

The Noah Project – Jewish Education, Celebration and Action for the Earth

British Jews formed an environmental group called The Noah Project in 1998. They chose the name Noah because he took the animals and birds into the ark, two by two. He was obeying God's command and preserving the biodiversity of the planet. A male and female could reproduce and save their species from extinction. The Noah Project works with other groups like Friends of the Earth to preserve the earth for future generations. They work on practical projects and also give 10 per cent of their profits to environmental work.

You can read more about The Noah Project's activities on www.noahproject.org.uk

Noah Project activities are very popular.

The Noah Project links its activities with three major Jewish festivals – Sukkot, Tu B'Shvat and Shavuot. Find out what connection these festivals have with the environment.

- How do Jews think the world began?
- Why do they say we must care for animals?
- How did The Noah Project get its name?

ACTIVITY A

Design your own logo for The Noah Project.

Muslims and the environment

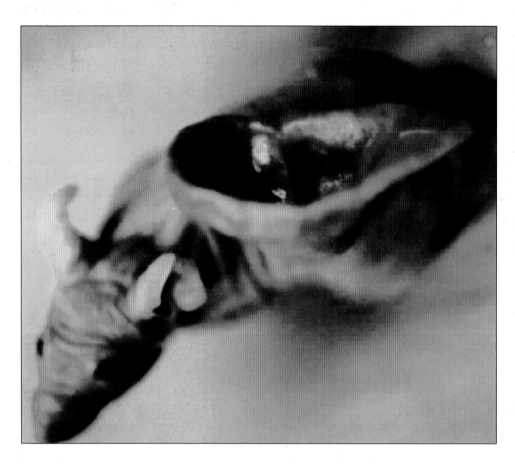

A mouse was developed to grow an ear that could be used by humans. Do you think Muslims would accept the use of animals to grow spare parts for humans? Do you feel it is right?

Creation

Muslims believe that Allah created everything in existence in six days. It was made out of nothing. That includes the universe with all its life – plant, animal and human. Muslims also believe Allah created other universes we have not yet discovered.

> I am placing on the earth one who shall rule as my deputy.
> The Qur'an

We have a duty to look after the planet. Muslims use the word Khalifa, which means steward or guardian of the earth. The holy book, the Qur'an, says that men and women are allowed to use God's creation for their needs. What they must not do is destroy it totally or damage it. Everybody is given free will to choose what they do, but on the Day of Judgement Allah will ask them how they have treated the earth.

The International Islamic University in Jordan treats conservation seriously because the Qur'an says it is a Muslim's duty to care for the environment. They are working on projects to restore forests destroyed in the First World War and researching water management and waste-water treatment.

Animals

Animals are Allah's creation so they should be treated with respect. Because Muslims believe people are Allah's greatest creation, animals can be used for human's needs. Animals can be killed for food but not for sport. Medical experiments on animals are permitted if there is no alternative but no animal should suffer unnecessarily.

'The world is green and beautiful and God has appointed you his steward over it. The whole earth has been created as a place of worship, pure and clean.'

Prophet Muhammad

This is one of the 99 names for Allah, Al-Khaliq, the Creator, God who creates everything out of nothing and knows what will happen to that life even before it begins.

'We are God's stewards and agents on earth. We are not masters of this earth; it does not belong to us to do what we wish. It belongs to God and he has entrusted us with its safekeeping... His trustees are responsible for maintaining the unity of His creation, the integrity of the earth, its flora and fauna, its wildlife and natural environment.'

Muslim Declaration on Nature

Camel story

One hot day as Muhammad was passing, he heard a camel bellowing and making terrible noises. On investigation he found a skinny animal tethered in the full sun without shade or water. Immediately Muhammad fetched it water and calmed the animal down. He looked round for the owner who was snoozing in the shade of a tree. Muhammad was furious. ' Allah has entrusted this animal to your care and what are you doing? Nothing! You're having a rest while this poor thing is suffering. On the Day of Judgement you will have to answer to Allah for this.'

It is God who has sovereignty over the heaven and the earth.

The Qur'an

- How do Muslims think the earth began?
- Why do Muslims believe people must treat animals well?
- Do Muslims have to be vegetarian or not?

Indeed your Lord is He who created the heavens and the earth in six days.

The Qur'an

ACTIVITY A

- Choose two quotations (or one long one) to display as a poster explaining why Muslims care about the environment. You may use magazine pictures on your poster or design the whole poster on computer.

- Find out about Islamic gardens. One important one you could research is the Alhambra in Spain.

- Role-play a discussion between a Muslim and a person who believes in fox-hunting.

'I have a mental picture of people sharing a massive banquet completely oblivious to the fact that the roof is crumbling and will eventually come crashing down on their heads. There are other people standing at the exits warning the diners to leave, but they take no notice – the meal is too good.'

F M Khalid writing about our attitude towards the environment

Sikhs and the environment

Creation

Karta Purakh, the creator of all things, is one name Sikhs use for God.

> In the beginning there was darkness:
> There was no earth or heaven, nothing but God's unequalled presence.
> There was no day or night or moon or sun
> No life, no voices, no wind, no water
> Neither creation nor destruction, nor the coming nor going.
> …When God wished it the world was created. Without support God created the firmament… By God's will the Lord has created the creation and watches over all.
>
> The Guru Granth Sahib

Sikhs say the creation process is far too complex for humans to understand.

> **The True Lord created the air**
> **Air gave birth to water,**
> **Water brought forth life**
> **And God himself is present in all the creation.**
>
> **The Guru Granth Sahib**

Consider this extract scientifically. Hydrogen and oxygen are present in the air. What is the chemical symbol for water? What is the current idea about where life began? Was it in the air, on land or in the water?

- Don't let magnificent animals become extinct.
- Above all, don't let human beings die of starvation and man-made disasters.
- Live and let live.
- For the sake of posterity, those countless generations of unborn children to come, let us save this Earth.
- Let us not misuse our privileges. Please don't let the songs of birds die.
- The earth is a garden. The Lord its gardener, cherishing all, none neglected.

from the sayings of Guru Nanak

Big fleas have little fleas upon their backs to bite 'em

Little fleas have smaller fleas and so ad infinitem.

What is the serious message behind this piece of fun? What examples can you think of where living beings depend on each other for their survival?

The perfect balance

Sikhs believe everything has its part to play in the smooth running of the universe, from the tiniest microscopic organism to the largest tree or animal. Trees produce oxygen which people need; people breathe out carbon dioxide which trees need. All is perfectly balanced. When we upset the balance there are problems. Global warming has shown that.

Sikhs believe that the natural world provides everything people need. God has designed it that way. That does not mean people have a right to grab the lot. They should only take what they need, no more. If they become greedy, then the balance of nature will be upset.

Tony Blair, the British Prime Minister, said in a speech on the environment in October 2000: 'The greatest threat to our environment today is climate change.' Would you agree? Can you think of other threats that might be worse? What were the reasons for these severe British floods in 2001? Do you think people brought the problem on themselves, or not?

- Discuss with your partner whether it matters if a species of plant or animal becomes extinct. Did the extinction of the dinosaurs cause any problems? Report your thoughts back to the class.

- Compare the Sikh creation story with the one in Genesis 1. In no more than 150 words, write about their similarities and differences.

- In what order do Sikhs think God created the world?

- Would Sikhs say people are allowed to take what they like from the world, or not?

- Which of Guru Nanak's sayings would be most useful today? Why?

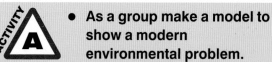

ACTIVITY **A**

- As a group make a model to show a modern environmental problem. The Geography Department may be able to give you information. Choose one of Guru Nanak's sayings as the title.

- Draw a diagram to show the balance of nature. Include a warning about what could happen when the balance is disturbed.

Hindus and the environment

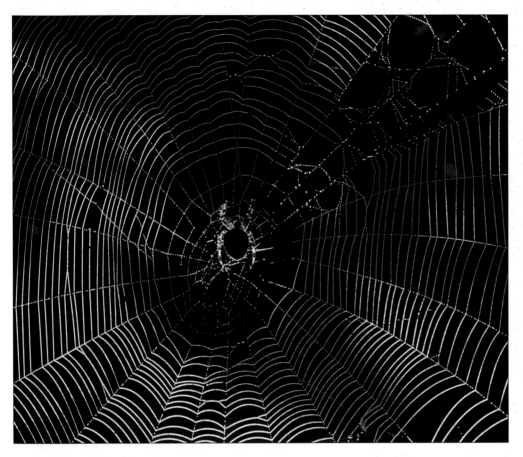

Hindus think this is a useful way of thinking about God and the universe. They believe that God creates the whole of the universe from himself, just as the spider spins the web out of its body. That means God is in nature. Everything we see around us is a part of God.

Creation

Hindus believe that God created the entire world, all the animals, plants and humans in it. Humans are superior to all other living things because they have been given the power of thought. They are also allowed to use nature for their needs.

Hindus see all living things are part of the same life cycle. If people try to take more than their share then nature becomes unbalanced. If we cut down all the trees or keep growing crops without nourishing the soil, then the land will not grow plants. We will go hungry. There are many stories in Hindu literature about living things working together. You might know the Ramayana story where Princess Sita's life is saved by the monkeys and the power of herbs.

> Every blade of grass, every drop of water, every breath of wind and every flame of fire is imbued with God.
>
> **Satish Kumar**

> The world has enough for everyone's need but not for everyone's greed.
>
> **Gandhi**

In pairs decide what Gandhi meant. Think about the terrible famine scenes you may have seen on television. Do you think Gandhi's words could explain those scenes or not?

Hindu pilgrims walk the seven-mile paths to see the groves where the god Krishna lived.

SAVING KRISHNA'S FORESTS

In the pilgrim town of Vrindavan, 80 miles south of Delhi, conservation work is afoot. Tradition has it that the god Krishna was born in the forest there. But in the 1980s the only sound to be heard was chainsaws.

Local engineer Sevak Sharan was horrified when he saw the last remaining large tree in the area being cut down. It was home to several peacocks. 'What was the use of my chanting and worship in the temples … if I couldn't protect these trees and animals which were part of my devotion,' he said.

He began a campaign to re-plant this sacred area. With the help of international bodies like the World Wildlife Fund, who pledged £25 000, the project began.

Seven miles of trees have now been planted round Vrindavan and along the path where two million pilgrims walk every year.

- What part do Hindus think God played in creation?
- Are humans and animals of equal worth to a Hindu?
- What do Hindus think happens when people exploit the natural resources of the world?

'If you walk gently over the earth, the earth will carry you.' What is the idea behind this Indian proverb?

ACTIVITY A

- Find out about the Hindu god Krishna, the most environmentally friendly of the gods.
- Role-play an interview between Sevak Sharan and the leader of the chainsaw gang during the 1980s.

Buddhists and the environment

Buddhists see the whole universe as a vast living entity. Humans, they believe, are only one part of the universe and not the rulers. Each part of the environment depends on another. Trees affect the soil, the climate and the lives of animals. In turn, the climate affects the soil and the animals.

> **Do you think humans, like animals, have any effect on the climate or the soil?**

There is no Buddhist creation story. Buddhists do not believe in a god, nor do they believe that the universe had a creator. They say that cosmic forces produced the environment and produced humans as well. It is all one big ecosystem. People should respect other life forms and live in peace with nature.

To be Buddhist is to be green

Buddhists try to live in harmony with nature. In a practical way that would mean using renewable power sources like the wind, waves and sun. Trees can be used so long as more are planted, although the Buddha himself remarked sadly on some people who cut down a tree after they had gratefully rested under it. 'Much like a friend the tree had given them shade,' he said.' To harm a friend is indeed an act of ingratitude.'

Modern Buddhists recycle materials as much as possible. Many also choose to be vegetarian out of respect for the life of animals. They buy or grow organic foods to avoid using pesticides that kill insects, harm the soil and humans.

> **What other things could Buddhists do in their daily lives to avoid destroying the planet?**

> As the bee takes the essence of a flower and flies away without destroying its beauty and perfume, so let the wise person travel through this life.

> **What does the quotation mean?**

Right livelihood

One important guideline Buddhists try to follow is called Right livelihood (see page 93). This means Buddhists should try to earn their living without harming other people, animals or the environment.

In 1992 a Tibetan Buddhist group bought Holy Island near the Isle of Arran in Scotland. The Buddhist monks respect the island's Christian origins and are working to create a self-sustaining environment. They began by planting 30 000 native trees. They are also building a retreat centre which will blend in with the natural surroundings. It is built into a hillside and has a turf roof. The windows face south to make use of solar power. Rainwater is caught and stored for use on the land but natural spring water is used for drinking and cooking. Waste water from the toilets is filtered in reed beds. The monks are planning to use wind power to generate electricity.

- **List five practical things a Buddhist could do that would show concern for the environment.**

- **Write a brief press release about the environmentally friendly life of the Buddhists on Holy Island.**

If possible they would choose jobs that help others in the natural world. It might be gardening or something that helps other people. Jobs like nursing, teaching, running a vegetarian restaurant or a health food shop would all help people.

What jobs do you think a Buddhist might consider was not a Right livelihood?

- **How do Buddhists explain the origins of the world?**

- **If they do not believe in a god why do Buddhists bother to care for the earth?**

Find out more about the Mongolian Buddhists' work to protect the rare snow leopard in their country. You could send an SAE to ARC, 3 Wynnstay Grove, Manchester, M14 6XG or look at their website www.religionsandconservation.org

Humanists and the environment

Humanists do not believe in a god. Humanism is called a life stance and not a religion. Humanists think the universe was the result of natural forces so they do not support any creation stories. Some prefer the scientific explanation that the world started with a big bang. Others argue that there never was a beginning as the universe consists of energy which continually expands and contracts.

Humanists believe life continually changes and evolves and as a result, human beings have become the most intelligent animal. Because Humanists say there is no god, they think people must take full responsibility for the planet and life on it. Humanists believe this is the only life we have so we should fulfill it. The earth is beautiful and we also depend on its natural resources for our existence. If we destroy the resources, we will destroy ourselves in the end.

The zoologist, Sir Julian Huxley, was a Humanist who helped set up London Zoo.
Find out more about him.

We value the environment, both natural and shaped by humanity, as the basis of life and a source of wonder and inspiration … and we accept our duty to maintain a sustainable environment for future generations.
We should care about the future of our planet because we care about other human beings, even those not born yet.

The last Dodo is thought to have died in the seventeenth century. It is said one species of plant or animal becomes extinct every day. Does that matter?

- **What can you discover about the Big Bang theory of creation?**

- **Why do Humanists think there is any need to concern themselves with the environment?**

- One leading Humanist was asked why he cared about the environment. He said, 'Because I want my grandchildren to be able to see elephants.' Write a paragraph to explain what he meant or whether you think this was a joke.

- In pairs discuss whether we ought be concerned about what may or may not happen in the future?

Humanists take their concern for the planet very seriously. Members of the Humanist Association have played leading parts in setting up groups to care for the environment. Societies like World Wide Fund for Nature, Friends of the Earth, Greenpeace and London Zoo included Humanists amongst their founders.

As a class discuss whether you think zoos are environmentally friendly or not.

Find out what species are currently being threatened with extinction. You could consult the British World Wildlife's website on www.wwf-uk.org, or the US site on www.worldwildlife.org or their international branch on www.panda.org which has a useful 'Just for Kids' section.

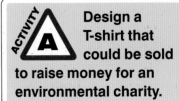

ACTIVITY A Design a T-shirt that could be sold to raise money for an environmental charity.

Religions working together for the environment

We are all in it together

Although the previous pages have looked at one religion at a time, many religions work with others to save the planet. In 1984 Prince Philip, the President of the World Wide Fund for Nature International (WWF), asked that different religious groups meet to find out what they could do about the problems that faced the planet. WWF invited the major world religions and other interested groups to talk.

The meeting took place in September 1986 on the twenty-fifth anniversary of WWF. Eight hundred people met in Assisi in Italy, where St Francis, a Christian saint who cared about animals, had lived.

Many came from religious groups but others belonged to no religion at all. All shared a concern for the future of the planet. The opening speaker said:

> We, members of major world religions and traditions, and men and women of good will, are gathered here, in this marvellous Church of St Francis, to awaken all people to their historical responsibility for the welfare of Planet Earth, our Sister and Mother, who in her generous sovereignty feeds us and all her creatures.

The gathering at Assisi in 1986.

Alliance of Religions and Conservation

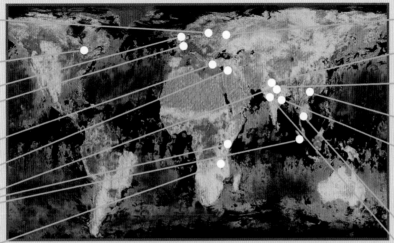

SOME PROJECTS SUPPORTED BY ARC

Syndesmos: Orthodox youth training at Valaam Monastery

First Nations' Faith and Ecology

Sacred Land

Solan Monastic farming

Orthodox environmental work camp, Mt Athos

Tel'Ada Monastery, Syria

The Ohito Declaration on Religion, Land and Conservation, Kenya and Malaysia

Zambia: educational development

Earth Charter Consultation

Anandpur Sikh development project

Vrindavan Conservation Project

Sacred Mountains of China

Jagannath Forest Project, Orissa

Muslim educational slide pack

Tree of Life: Buddhist education pack

Palitana Jain greening project

ARC also works in association with the World Faiths and Development Dialogue

The Assisi meeting was so successful that people wanted to continue the work. In 1995 they held a Summit of Religions and Conservation at Windsor Castle. Many practical projects were started and a group was formed to co-ordinate all the activities.

It was called the Alliance of Religions and Conservation, known as ARC. Many of the projects you have been reading about on earlier pages are ones which ARC have aided.

To discover more about ARC's current projects look at their website:www.religionsandconservation.org

- Whose idea was it that all the religions should meet together and talk about environmental issues?

- Why was Assisi chosen for the first meeting?

Find out when St Francis lived and what his connection is with the environment.

ACTIVITY A Design a folded A4 leaflet that could be given to visitors to one of the conservation sites shown here.

Who else cares about the planet?

Many people who are Humanist or have no religious beliefs are sure the environment matters. They have grouped together to make their message stronger. The two large organisations shown here have supporters from all religions and people with no faith. All care deeply about the planet. There are many, many more organisations. You might like to find out about a different one that supports a cause you care deeply about.

Friends of the Earth

What do you think their message 'For the planet for the people' means?

Friends of the Earth

about **Friends of the Earth**

Here are **five easy ways** to help make your **environment** a cleaner, greener place.

1 Use less paper and always buy recycled paper products. Encourage your school or college to do so too.

Ancient forests are being destroyed to make way for tree factories for the paper industry.

2 Refuse unnecessary packaging; reuse things like envelopes, bags and containers; get your household to recycle as much as possible. If there aren't enough recycling facilities ask your Council for more.

We throw away 27 million tonnes of rubbish from our homes every year in the UK.

3 Take showers instead of baths. Use your washing up water on your plants! Write to your water company urging them to stop wasting water.

Rocketing demand for water is putting severe pressure on important wildlife habitats.

4 Walk, cycle and use public transport whenever possible. Let your MP know you want him/her to support measures to reduce traffic.

Every year up to 24,000 people in the UK die prematurely because of air pollution, mainly due to traffic fumes.

5 Get your household to replace its three most-used light bulbs with low-energy, compact fluorescent light bulbs. Write to the company that supplies your electricity asking what they are doing to develop cleaner energy sources and help your household save energy.

The energy we use at home causes more than a quarter of the UK's climate-changing carbon dioxide pollution.

Greenpeace works internationally to change things for the better.

we've had many successes

> Our campaigning has seen all major UK supermarkets remove GM ingredients from their own-brand food.

> We developed 'Greenfreeze', the first ozone and climate friendly fridge.

> Our campaigning has ensured a total ban on the dumping of all oil installations in European waters.

> We've ensured that the Great Bear Rainforest in Canada is not destroyed by logging companies.

> We've secured a ban on 'Wall of Death' driftnets in European waters saving thousands of dolphins and other marine wildlife.

> We've ensured a 50-year ban on mineral exploitation in Antarctica.

WITH YOUR HELP WE CAN
ACHIEVE SO MUCH MORE

Greenpeace

The aim of Greenpeace is clear from its name: 'Green' because they care about the environment, 'Peace' because they believe in non-violent direct action. Look back to the idea of peaceful protest on page 40. Greenpeace was started in 1971 when some North Americans protested about nuclear testing off the coast of Alaska.

List the different causes that Greenpeace has campaigned for. Can you work out what each picture relates to?

Do you have to believe in God to care about the environment?

ACTIVITY A

Design a questionnaire to see what people think. This can be a computer spreadsheet if you wish. Some of the questions you will need to ask are:

● Do you believe in God? (Answer Yes or No)

● Do you think you personally should care for the environment? (Answer Yes or No)

● Ask them to give reasons for their beliefs and briefly write them down.

● You may include other questions but try to keep the questionnaire simple enough for you to record the responses.

● Try to question people from a wide age range, e.g. young, middle-aged, and elderly. Include a column where you can record to which age group the participants belonged.

● Question at least 20 people.

● Analyse your results to see if the statement is true.

● Write a brief report giving reasons for the results of your survey.

1 Name two charities that are helping the environment and describe what they are doing.
2 'People are stewards of the earth.' What does that mean?
3 Do you think belief in God makes any difference to the way we treat the planet?
4 Write a press release about the way one religion, or Humanism, is helping the environment.
5 Role-play a television interview with someone from the local Green Group who is concerned about the proposed landfill site in a bluebell wood.
6 Work in groups of three or four. Design a poster to show what your school could do for the environment. Make sure you tell people why they should bother.

GOING FORWARD

1 Describe or draw a scene on earth in 2100 and label what is happening. Areas you might think about are: air quality, the state of the sea and beaches, what animals are around, global warming.
2 Find out what the Gaia theory is and write down your information.
3 Plan an assembly.
- Make people aware of the damage that is being done to the planet.
- Explain why they should be concerned.
- Tell them about one religion's work for the environment.
- Suggest some practical things they could do.

"Never again will we stand on the threshold of a new age. We that are here now are touched in some mysterious way With the ability to change And make the future"

Ben Okri calls his poem 'Mental Fight – an anti-spell for the twenty-first century.' What do you think he is trying to say to us? Compose your own message for the planet in the twenty-first century.